THE POETRY HOME REPAIR MANUAL

The Poetry Home Repair Manual

Practical Advice for Beginning Poets

TED KOOSER

UNIVERSITY OF NEBRASKA PRESS ➡ LINCOLN & LONDON

Acknowledgments for previously
published material appear on
pages 159–63, which constitute
an extension of the copyright page.

♾

Library of Congress Cataloging-in-
Publication Data
Kooser, Ted.
The poetry home repair manual :
practical advice for beginning
poets / Ted Kooser.
p. cm.
Includes bibliographical references.
ISBN 0-8032-2769-8 (cl.: alk. paper)
1. Poetry—Authorship.   I. Title.
PN1059.A9K66 2005
808.1–dc22
2004024700

Charles Levendosky,
poet and citizen
1936–2004

CONTENTS

ACKNOWLEDGMENTS

Special thanks to my wife, Kathleen Rutledge, expert editor and wise counsel. My gratitude to Susan Aizenberg, Steve Cox, Susan Firer, George Garrett, Jeff Gundy, Bob King, Jeff Daniel Marion, Linda Parsons Marion, David Mason, Leonard and Carol Nathan, Luan Pitsch, Christine Stewart-Nunez, and Don Welch, who read the manuscript and provided helpful comments. Thanks also to my editor, Ladette Randolph, and her continuing generosity toward my writing. Thanks also to my students at the University of Nebraska, whose efforts to write poetry have shaped some of what I offer in these pages.

Most of a poet's education is self-education, and most of what you'll learn you'll teach yourself through reading and writing poems. A good teacher may be able to nudge you along, may assign exercises like the how-to poem or the poem-in-answer-to-a-question, but eventually you'll get tired of doing literary sit-ups and knee bends and grow impatient to write the poems you *really* want to write, poems you feel inside you, poems like those you find in the books of writers you admire.

But the craft of careful writing and meticulous revision *can* be taught. *The Poetry Home Repair Manual* can assist you in making your poems stronger and more effective in finding an audience. I've been writing and publishing poetry for more than forty years, and in these pages I offer you some of my favorite tools for tuning up the poems you write. I'm confident you'll find them useful.

This is only one of many books about poetry writing. It's not very lengthy because there's only so much I know. I've learned a lot about writing poems, but I'll never get to the end of all the poetry still to be learned from, never make all the discoveries I'd like to make.

You'll find I pay lots of attention to a poet's relationship with readers. If you've gotten the impression from teachers or from reading contemporary poetry that poets don't need to write with a sense of somebody out there who might read what they've written, this book is not for you. Poetry is communication, and every word I've written here subscribes to that belief. Poetry's purpose is to reach other people and to touch their hearts. If a poem doesn't make sense to anybody but its author, nobody but its author will care a whit about it. That doesn't mean that your poems can't be cryptic, or elusive, or ambiguous if that's how you want to write, as long as you keep in mind that there's somebody on the other end of the communication. I favor poems that keep the obstacles between you and that person to a minimum. My approach is open to argument, of course, but even if you disagree with me on every page, even if I make you angry, I'm pretty sure you'll take away something worthwhile from what you find here.

My writing philosophy owes much to an idea that Lewis Hyde expresses in his book *The Gift: Imagination and the Erotic Life of Property*. He suggests that those who are gifted should give something back. With Hyde's thought resounding in my head and my own need to feel useful, I've shaped my own philosophy of writing, in particular a belief that people who have the ability to write have an obligation to offer something of use to their chosen readers. I emphasize *chosen* readers; later in this book I'll talk at length about the process of choosing your audience through the use of imaginary readers.

Throughout this book I cite examples of poems. Nearly all of these were written in recent years. There's much to be said in favor of studying the poetry of the past, but I want to direct your attention to poems being written *today*. It's the *now* of poetry you plan to enter, offering your own poems.

The poet John Ciardi once said that whenever in time, and wherever in the universe, any person speaks or writes in any detail about the technical management of a poem, the resulting irascibility of the reader's response is a constant. I hope I won't exhaust your patience.

CHAPTER ONE

A Poet's Job Description

Before we get to the specifics or writing and revision, let me say a few things about the job you're taking on.

A CAREER AS A POET?

You'll never be able to make a living writing poems. We'd better get this money business out of the way before we go any further. I don't want you to have any illusions. You might make a living as a teacher of poetry writing or as a lecturer about poetry, but writing poems won't go very far toward paying your electric bill. A poem published in one of the very best literary magazines in the country might net you a check for enough money to buy half a sack of groceries. The chances are much better that all you'll receive, besides the pleasure of seeing your poem in print, are a couple of copies of the magazine, one to keep and one to show to your mother. You might get a letter or postcard from a grateful reader, always a delightful surprise. But look at it this way: Any activity that's worth lots of money, like professional basketball, comes with rules pinned all over it. In poetry, the only rules worth thinking about are the standards of perfection you set for yourself.

There's no money in poetry because most of my neighbors, and most of yours, don't have any use for it. If, at a neighborhood yard sale, you happened to find the original handwritten manuscript of T. S. Eliot's "The Waste Land," you could take it to every quick shop in your city and you wouldn't find a single person who would trade you ten gallons of gas for it.

Part of the reason for our country's lack of interest in poetry is that most of us learned in school that finding the meaning of a poem is way too much work, like cracking a walnut and digging out the meat. Most readers have plenty to do that's far more interesting than puzzling over poems. I'll venture that 99 percent of the people who read the *New Yorker* prefer the cartoons to the poems.

A lot of this resistance to poetry is to be blamed on poets. Some go out of their way to make their poems difficult if not downright discouraging. That may be because difficult poems are what they think they're expected to write to advance their careers. They know it's the professional interpreters of poetry—book reviewers and literary critics—who most often establish a poet's reputation, and that those interpreters are attracted to poems that offer opportunities to show off their skills at interpretation. A poet who writes poetry that doesn't require explanation, who writes clear and accessible poems, is of little use to critics building their own careers as interpreters. But a clear and accessible poem *can* be of use to an everyday reader.

It is possible to nourish a small and appreciative audience for poetry if poets would only think less about the reception of critics and more about the needs of readers. *The Poetry Home Repair Manual* advocates for poems that can be read and understood without professional interpretation. My teacher and mentor, Karl Shapiro, once pointed out that the poetry of the twentieth century was the first poetry *that had to be taught*. He might have said *that had to be explained*. I believe with all my heart that it's a virtue to show our appreciation for readers by writing with kindness, generosity, and humility toward them. Everything you'll read here holds to that.

One other point: Isaac Newton attributed his accomplishments to standing on the shoulders of giants. He meant great thinkers who had gone before. Accordingly, beginning poets sometimes start off trying to stand on the shoulders of famous poets, imitating the difficult and obscure poems those successful poets have published. That's understandable, but they soon learn that, somehow, no literary journal is interested in publishing their difficult poems. If these beginners were to study the careers of the famous poets upon whose work they're modeling their own, they'd find that those writers were often, in their early years, publishing clear, understandable poems. In most instances, only after establishing reputations could they go on to write in more challenging ways. In a sense they earned the right to do so by first attracting an audience of readers, editors, and publishers with less difficult poems.

THE TWO POETS

We serve each poem we write. We make ourselves subservient to our poetry. Any well-made poem is worth a whole lot more to the world than the person who wrote it. In one of Tomas Transtömer's poems he says, "Fantastic to see how my poem is growing / while I myself am shrinking. / It's getting bigger, it's taking my place."

There's an essential difference between *being a poet* and *writing poetry*. There are, in a sense, two poets, the one alone writing a poem and the one in the black turtleneck and beret, trying to look sexy. Here's an older poem of mine:

➡ A POETRY READING

> Once you were young along a river, tree to tree,
> with sleek black wings and red shoulders.
> You sang for yourself but all of them listened to you.
>
> Now you're an old blue heron with yellow eyes
> and a gray neck tough as a snake.
> You open your book on its spine, a split fish,
> and pick over the difficult ribs,
> turning your better eye down to the work
> of eating your words as you go.

At the beginning, too often it's the idea of *being* a poet that matters most. It's those sexy black wings and red shoulders. It's the *attention* you want, as the poem says, "all of them listening to you." And then you grow old and, if you are lucky, grow wise.

I'm in my sixties, but I too was once young and felt flashy as a red-winged blackbird. I don't remember the specific date when I decided to be a poet, but it was during one of my many desperately lonely hours as a teenager, and I set about establishing myself as a poet with adolescent single-mindedness. I began to dress the part. I took to walking around in rubber shower sandals and white beachcomber pants that tied with a piece of clothesline rope. I let my hair grow longer and tried to grow a beard. I carried big fat books wherever I went—like Adolph Harnack's

Outlines of the History of Dogma and Kierkegaard's *Fear and Trembling*. I couldn't have understood a word of these books if I'd tried, but they looked really good clenched under my arm and, as a bonus, helped me look as if I had big biceps.

There were, it seemed to me, many benefits accruing to a career as a poet. There were fame and immortality: the lichen-encrusted bust of the poet on his monument in the town cemetery, standing throughout time in a swirl of autumn leaves. There was also the delicious irresponsibility of the bohemian lifestyle: No more picking up my room, no more mowing the yard.

But best of all was the adoration of women. *That* was what I was most interested in. In those years I desperately needed some sort of a gimmick, for I was thin and pimply, my palms sweated, and my breath was sour from smoking the Chesterfields that despite the claims of magazine advertising had failed to make me irresistible.

I got the idea that being a poet might make me attractive by reading *Life* magazine, which occasionally profiled some rumpled, unshaven, melancholy poet (never a female poet, as far as I can remember), and I got the idea from the accompanying text that these guys were "lady-killers," as people used to say. I especially remember a photograph of grizzled old John Berryman surrounded by dewy-eyed college women, a smile on his lips. It had to be the poetry that made the difference, I figured, because were it not for that, disheveled old Berryman wouldn't likely have gotten to first base with the women.

It didn't occur to me for a long time that in order to earn the title of Poet, I ought to have written at least one poem. To me, the writing of poetry didn't have all that much to do with it. Being a poet was looking the part.

I was an artificial poet, a phony, when, by rubbing shoulders with poetry, I gradually became interested in writing it. I'd begun to carry books less cumbersome than Harnack and Kierkegaard, and one day I picked up the New Directions paperback edition of William Carlos Williams's *Selected Poems*. It weighed no more than a few ounces and fit in my pocket. I began to read Williams and soon discovered other poets whose work I liked: May Swenson, Randall Jarrell, John Crowe Ransom, to name a few. I began to read poetry whenever I had a moment free from pretending to be a poet, and soon I started to write a few poems of my own. The two sides of being a poet—the poet as celebrity and the poet as writer—began to fall into balance. I read poems, I wrote poems, and at times, sometimes for hours on end, I was able to forget about trying to attract women.

Today I read poems, I write poems, and at times, yes, sometimes for hours on end, I forget about women. Yet there are still the two poets present, the one who quietly concentrates on perfecting the poem and the one who wants more than anything else to be celebrated and adored. I'm delighted and nourished by the first poet and embarrassed by the second.

Poetry is a lot more important than poets.

TOO MANY POETS?

A noted contemporary poet and critic has said we ought to keep poetry a secret from the masses. Another, the editor of a prestigious anthology of poetry, said that each nation ought to have no more than a handful of poets. Both sound pretty elitist, don't they? Well, we'll always have among us those who think the best should be reserved for the few. Considering the ways in which so many of us waste our time, what would be wrong with a world in which *everybody* were writing poems? After all, there's a significant service to humanity in spending time doing no harm. While you're writing your poem, there's one less scoundrel in the world. And I'd like a world, wouldn't you, in which people actually took time to think about what they were saying? It would be, I'm certain, a more peaceful, more reasonable place. I don't think there could ever be too many poets. By writing poetry, even those poems that fail and fail miserably, we honor and affirm life. We say "We loved the earth but could not stay."

ISN'T IT DIFFICULT TO FIND ACCEPTANCE?

What makes the work of a poet most difficult is not that the world doesn't always appreciate what he or she does. We all know how wrong the world can be. It was wrong about Vincent Van Gogh when it refused to purchase his sunflower painting for the roughly $125 he was asking, and it is every bit as wrong to pay $35 million or $40 million for it today.

What is most difficult for a poet is to find the time to read and write when there are so many distractions, like making a living and caring for others. But the time set aside for being a poet, even if only for a few moments each day, can be wonderfully happy, full of joyous, solitary discovery.

Here's a passage about the joy of making art from Louise Nevelson's memoir *Dawns and Dusks*. Nevelson was a sculptor, but what she says about an artist's life can be applied to poetry, too: "I'd rather work twenty-four hours a day in my studio and come in here and fall down on the bed than do anything I know. Because it is living. It's like pure water; it's living. The essence of living is in doing, and in doing, I have made my world and it's a much better world than I ever saw outside."

The essence of living is in doing, Nevelson suggests, and the essence of being a poet is in the writing, not in the publications or the prizes.

BEING OF SERVICE

The Nobel Prize–winning poet Seamus Heaney, writing on William Butler Yeats, said (the emphasis is mine), "The aim of the poet and the poetry is finally *to be of service*, to ply the effort of the individual work into the larger work of the community as a whole." That's good enough to cut out and pin up over your typewriter.

In the following poem, ostensibly a description of a street scene, one of my favorite poets suggests something about serving, about how a single poem can alter the way in which a reader sees the world.

➽ FIRE BURNING IN A FIFTY-FIVE GALLON DRUM

Next time you'll notice them on your way to work
or when you drive by that place near the river
where the stockyards used to stand, where everything

is gone now. They'll be leaning over the edge
of the barrel, getting it started—they'll step back
suddenly, and hold out their hands, as though

something fearful had appeared at its center.
Others will be coming over by then, pulling up
handfuls of weeds, bringing sticks and bits of paper,

laying them in gently, offering them to something
still hidden deep down inside the drum.
They will all form a circle, their hands almost

touching, sparks rising through their fingers,
their faces bright, their bodies darkened by smoke,
by flakes of ash swirling around them in the wind.

Look at the first five words of this poem by Jared Carter: *Next time
you'll notice them.* We're likely to breeze right past a phrase like that
without thinking much about it, aren't we? By habit, we tend to look
toward the end of a poem for the BIG revelations, the BIG messages,
but that's not what happens here.

For me, those first five words are among the most important in
the poem. Why? Because Carter is to some degree writing about the
relationship between a poet and his readers, about the gift a poet gives
an audience. Those few words make an important assertion: Once we
have read and been affected by a poem, our awareness of its subject—in
this instance a group of men huddled around a barrel—may be forever
heightened and made memorable. With the confidence of someone
who knows the effects of reading poetry, Carter suggests that it's likely
that readers of his poem will never again pass a group of men warming
themselves at a barrel of fire without a sense of heightened awareness.
We are thus indelibly marked by the poems we read, and the more
poems we read the deeper is our knowledge of the world.

Though it can be a lovely experience to write a poem that pleases
and delights its author, to write something that touches a reader is just
about as good as it gets. The finest compliment I've ever received came
from a woman who had read a little poem of mine called "Spring
Plowing" in which I describe a family of mice moving their nests
out of a field to avoid a farmer's plow. The poem presents a playful,
Walt Disney–like scene, with the mice carrying tiny lanterns, and
the oldest among them loudly lamenting their arduous journey. This
woman wrote to me and said that she would never again pass a freshly
plowed field in spring without thinking about those mice. I'd given
her something that changed the way she saw the world, and she was
thankful for that. I was deeply honored.

Poems that change our perceptions are everywhere you look, and one

of the definitions of poetry might be that a poem freshens the world.
Take a look at this little landscape by A. R. Ammons:

➥ WINTER SCENE

There is now not a single
leaf on the cherry tree:

except when the jay
plummets in, lights, and,

in pure clarity, squalls:
then every branch

quivers and
breaks out in blue leaves.

After letting that poem become part of your experience, will you ever be
able to look at a blue jay landing in a bare tree without a special sense
of recognition? As Jared Carter says, "Next time you'll notice them on
your way to work."

That's the kind of thing you can give readers with your poems, a
re-freshening of the world.

And just to show you that your gift—the *refreshment* you serve up to
your readers—can come as a very small serving, here's a one-line poem
by Joseph Hutchison:

➥ ARTICHOKE

O heart weighed down by so many wings

Could you ever look at an artichoke in the same way after reading that?

There's a toy much like a kaleidoscope but without the colored chips.
Like a kaleidoscope it consists of a mirrored tube. You look through it
and see whatever is at the other end. Turn it toward just about anything
and what's beyond you becomes more interesting. This is how some
poems work. The poem is the device through which the ordinary world
is seen in a new way—engaging, compelling, even beautiful.

READING TO WRITE

The best way to learn the art of writing poetry is to read as much of it as
possible—contemporary poems, ancient poems, folk poems, poems

in translation, light verse, nonsense verse, song lyrics, jingles, poems of every kind. Every successful poem acknowledges the influence of other poems. Every unsuccessful poem illustrates by its failures what might have been better if its author had read a little more poetry.

It takes only a little time to read a few poems each day, from literary journals, from books. If you have a computer, thousands of poems are accessible online. It just takes a little initiative to develop a daily reading habit. I make a practice of reading some poetry before I sit down to write. It helps me to get my mind tilted in the right direction. That might work for you, too, but whatever routine you choose, the important thing is to get in the habit of reading poems and thinking about what you've read.

Every poet learns to write by imitation, just as every painter learns to paint by looking at paintings. Every composer learns to write music by studying the music of other composers. Read anybody's first poem and you'll see there was a model for it. That influence might have been a rollicking Robert Service ballad or a maudlin greeting card jingle, but you can tell the poet got the idea of what a poem *is* from somewhere else, from reading another poem.

It can be helpful to type out the poems you like, or to pencil them into a notebook. This can assist you in understanding how good poems are constructed.

We teach ourselves to write the kinds of poems we like to read. The more poems you read, and the more models you learn from and imitate, the better your writing will get. After you have read lots of poetry and written lots of poetry, your own work will become more accomplished and more your own, such a rich porridge of everything you've read and experimented with that most readers won't be able to separate the ingredients. To that, you add your personality, character, and experience and, *presto*, you've got your own way of writing, your *style*, a uniqueness born of hands-on work with reading and writing.

Most poets can recall some early reading experience that triggered their interest in writing. For example, I first read Walter de la Mare's poem "The Listeners" when I was thirteen or fourteen, and I've never quite recovered. "The Listeners" was in a junior high English textbook, and my class discussed it at great length, puzzling over its mystery. It's about an anonymous horseman who stops by a darkened house one night, pounds on the door, and calls out to the absent occupants. Nobody answers his knock, but inside the house are ghostly listeners.

> But only a host of phantom listeners
> That dwelt in the lone house then
> Stood listening in the quiet of the moonlight
> To that voice from the world of men:
> Stood thronging the faint moonbeams on the dark stair,
> That goes down to the empty hall,
> Hearkening in an air stirred and shaken
> By the lonely Traveler's call.

"The lonely Traveler's call!" How that resonated with me as an adolescent! I thought, *Hey, I too am a lonely traveler!*

Alone in the cold and the dark the traveler senses a consciousness waiting behind the door:

> he felt in his heart their strangeness,
> Their stillness answering his cry

He knocks again, and then:

> he suddenly smote on the door, even
> Louder and lifted his head:—
> "Tell them I came, and no one answered,
> That I kept my word," he said.

Then he gallops away:

> Never the least stir made the listeners,
> Though every word he spake
> Fell echoing through the shadowiness of the still house
> From the one man left awake:
> Ay, they heard his foot upon the stirrup,
> And the sound of iron on stone,
> And how the silence surged softly backward
> When the plunging hoofs were gone.

What was the relationship of the phantom listeners to the horseman?

Who were they? Why did the horseman feel obligated to stop and knock? What did he owe the listeners?

My own poem "Abandoned Farmhouse," written when I was about thirty years old, is taught today to students who are about the age I was when I first read "The Listeners," and I've learned from their letters that they puzzle over my poem in just the same way my class puzzled over de la Mare's. (Throughout this book, I frequently use my own poems as examples. I'm not putting my work forward as being superior to that of others. It's just that I know a lot about how my poems got written, what went into them, and what happened while I was trying to make them better.)

➻ ABANDONED FARMHOUSE

He was a big man, says the size of his shoes
on a pile of broken dishes by the house;
a tall man too, says the length of the bed
in an upstairs room; and a good, God-fearing man,
says the bible with a broken back
on the floor below a window, dusty with sun;
but not a man for farming, say the fields
cluttered with boulders and the leaky barn.

A woman lived with him, say the bedroom wall
papered with lilacs and the kitchen shelves
covered with oilcloth, and they had a child,
says the sandbox made from a tractor tire.
Money was scarce, say the jars of plum preserves
and canned tomatoes sealed in the cellar hole,
and the winters cold, say the rags in the window frames.
It was lonely here, says the narrow country road.

Something went wrong, says the empty house
in the weed-choked yard. Stones in the fields
say he was not a farmer; the still-sealed jars
in the cellar say she left in a nervous haste.
And the child? Its toys are strewn in the yard
like branches after a storm—a rubber cow,
a rusty tractor with a broken plow,
a doll in overalls. Something went wrong, they say.

Almost every year I receive a letter or two from middle school students somewhere in the country asking me what it was that *really* happened to the people in that farmhouse. Were they abducted by aliens? Were they attacked by a motorcycle gang?

What I was thinking when I wrote the poem, and what in error I thought would be obvious, was that the man, the head of the household, had failed at farming and with his family had abandoned the farm, perhaps because of creditors, perhaps seeking an opportunity somewhere else. There's an important lesson here: *Once your poems are out of your reach, you won't be there to explain your intentions to your readers.*

There's something to be said for mystery, if handled with care: A little mystery can help make a poem memorable. Too much mystery, though, and you'll discourage most readers.

"The Listeners" has continued to influence my writing. In at least a dozen of my poems written over the past forty years you can find me beating on doors and hollering out to the ghosts within. I am in many ways still the Lone Traveler, there on the stoop, a lump in my throat as I holler out, " 'Tell them I came, . . . / That I kept my word.' "

Critics don't take De la Mare's poem seriously today; it doesn't offer enough challenges. How could anyone write a thesis on "The Listeners"? The poem is puzzling enough for middle schoolers but not puzzling enough for a twenty-page essay, let alone a PhD dissertation. But I offer you my experience as an example of how one poem can linger throughout a long writing life. You too will take away something from every poem you read. If you can find time to read for as little as fifteen minutes a day, every day, every poem you read—every word *about* poetry you read—will be worth your time. And believe it or not, you'll learn almost as much from poorly written poems as from the most accomplished. When you find a poem you think is a terrible mess, ask yourself how it could have been made better.

A CORNER OF YOUR OWN

For reading and writing you'll need time alone. The work and study of writing happens not in the company of others but in solitude. True, it can be helpful for beginning poets to talk about their work with other writers, but no writing group or poetry workshop will get your poems written. It may be lots of fun to sit in a coffeehouse wearing your favorite beret and smoking Camels in a long holder and chatting about poems and poets with your friends, but if you're going to write, you need to go home and write.

Writing can be exhilarating work. While you sit quietly scribbling into your notebook, memories and associations rise like bubbles out of the thick mud of your mind. Interesting words pop up, colorful images. It's a kind of play, and there's a lot of happiness in it. Karl Shapiro, whom I mentioned earlier, once wrote that the proper response to a work of art is joy, even hilarity. By that he meant responding not only to works of art by others, but to one's own work as well. There's nothing wrong with delighting in what you do. In fact, *most of the fun you'll have as a poet will come about during the process of writing*. Eventual publication and recognition are reasons to feel good about yourself and your work, of course, but to keep going you'll learn to find pleasure working at your desk, out of the way of the world. One of my first writing places was a cardboard refrigerator box pushed into the corner of the bedroom in a tiny apartment my first wife and I rented while I was in graduate school. I sat in the box to write my poems, and taped the drafts on the cardboard walls. You too can make a place to write. Your poems will be the records of the discoveries you make while writing in that place.

BUT HOW DO YOU COME UP WITH IDEAS?

The poet Jane Hirshfield wrote: "A work of art defines itself into being, when we awaken into it and by it, when we are moved, altered, stirred. It feels as if we have done nothing, only given it a little time, a little space; some hairline-narrow crack opens in the self, and there it is." She goes on to quote Kafka: "You do not even have to leave your room. Remain sitting at your table and listen. Do not even listen, simply wait. Do not even wait, remain still and solitary. The world will freely offer itself to you unasked. It has no choice. It will roll in ecstasy at your feet."

You sit with your notebook, and after a while something begins to interest you. The poet William Stafford described it as being like fishing: you throw out your line and wait for a little tug. Maybe all you get is a minnow, three or four words that seem to have a little magic, but even that can be enough to get the writing started. And a minnow can be pretty good bait for bigger fish.

As to *ideas* for poems, well . . . though there have been plenty of poets who've set out to wrap ideas in verse, many of those poems look just that way, like ideas wrapped in verse. They look as if they had been willed into being. It takes a big mind like John Milton's or Matthew Arnold's to wrap up an idea and make a good poem, and most of us just aren't that smart.

I can't speak for all the poets writing today, but I suspect that the freshest and most engaging poems most often don't come from *ideas* at all. Ideas are orderly, rational, and to some degree logical. They come clothed in complete sentences, like "Overpopulation is the cause of all the problems in the world." Instead, poems are triggered by catchy twists of language or little glimpses of life. The poet's ideas might emerge while he or she is playfully writing about, say, the appearance of a stack of storm windows lying in the grass or the way in which a praying mantis turns her head to look at the mate she's about to eat. The poet's ideas, his or her reasoned assessments of the world, emerge through the poetry whether intended or not.

When something happens to catch your attention, and you feel like making a note of it, you can usually trust your impulse. There may well be something there worth writing about. Chances are good that you've noticed whatever it is because somewhere within you, you have a glimmer of feeling about it. At first you may not recognize or be able to elucidate that emotion, but as you work with your words the feelings can be expected to come forward.

For example, a friend recently sent me a newsletter for people who like to fish. In it there was a lot of talk about the levels of water dropping in midwestern lakes because of drought. One article noted that the tops of Christmas trees thrown into a lake for habitat were beginning to stick out of the water and that when people tried to move them into deeper water, schools of little crappies fell out of their branches. That caught me, and even though I can't identify my feelings about it just yet, if I were to start writing about those branches full of glittering fish my feelings would gradually emerge. Later in the book I talk about writing about feelings, but for now let me say that unless you care at least just a little about your subject, you're not going to write very well about it.

The poet Richard Hugo, in his book *The Triggering Town*, said that often the original impulse for the poem gets dropped along the way, and something entirely unthought of begins to emerge. I've had that happen, and you will too.

Here's a poem of mine, written after noticing how a woman in a wheelchair used her hands to propel it along. I originally set out merely to describe that motion.

➥ A RAINY MORNING

A young woman in a wheelchair,
wearing a black nylon poncho spattered with rain,
is pushing herself through the morning.
You have seen how pianists
sometimes bend forward to strike the keys,
then lift their hands, draw back to rest,
then lean again to strike just as the chord fades.
Such is the way this woman
strikes at the wheels, then lifts her long white fingers,
letting them float, then bends again to strike
just as the chair slows, as if into a silence.
So expertly she plays the chords
of this difficult music she has mastered,
her wet face beautiful in its concentration,
while the wind turns the pages of rain.

Somebody might conclude that the *idea* of this poem is that the disabled are courageous and should be honored, and of course I *do* think the disabled are courageous and should be honored, but the poem was not written with that in mind. In fact, I couldn't have begun to compose a poem *about* the courage of the disabled, which is a big, complex idea. For me, meaning arrives almost unbidden from an accumulation of specific details. I was simply struck by how much the movement of the woman's hands was like that of someone playing a piano. That's where I started. Sure, my thoughts about courage can be drawn from the finished poem, but they were not the core about which the poem was formed.

It's through the process of writing that ideas and feelings emerge. Let yourself play with whatever you observe. Describe a pot boiling on the stove, the flash of bicycle spokes. What you think and feel about the world can be trusted to surface.

And don't think you have to have an IQ of 160 to write good poems. Most of the poets I know are of average intelligence. What makes them "different" is that they love playing with language.

WORK AND REWORK AND REWORK

After you've written your first drafts, you begin to revise, making critical judgments about what you've written, decisions based in part upon which word goes best in which position, about the appropriateness of a figure of speech, about the use of grammar and punctuation, and about how your writing may affect an imagined reader. Revision, and I mean *extensive* revision, is the key to transforming a mediocre poem into a work that can touch and even alter a reader's heart. It's the biggest part of the poet's job description. I've published hundreds of poems, most of them less than twenty lines in length, and people are always surprised to learn that I might take a single short poem through twenty, or thirty, or even forty versions before I think it's finished. Linda Pastan, an award-winning writer whose poems are frequently less than a page in length, said in a radio interview that some of her poems go though a hundred revisions. It's been my preference to revise toward clarity and freshness, and I hope that after I have labored over my poems for many hours they look as if they'd been dashed off in a few minutes, the way good watercolor paintings look. But that's the way I choose to write my poems. You'll want to follow your own preferences.

Much has been written about revision, but I've always liked this passage from Edward Weeks's book *This Trade of Writing*:

> A. Edward Newton tells a story of Oscar Wilde at an English house party. Pleading the necessity of working while the humor was on, he begged to be excused from joining the other guests. In the evening his hostess asked him what he had accomplished, "This morning," he said, "I put a comma in one of my poems." Surprised, the lady inquired whether the afternoon's work had been equally exhausting. "Yes," said Wilde, passing his hand wearily over his brow, "this afternoon I took it out again." Every

writer worth rereading has suffered from this backing-and-filling process. . . . When the ideas begin to run smoothly they can so easily run away with us, leaving behind pages which in a colder mood seem full of extravagance. In the heat of composition it is not wise to halt for precision; that must come later, the search for the exact word, the smooth transition, the terse phrase that will save half a page. . . . Revision is the worst possible drudgery; yet no book has been made full and rich without it.

Though Weeks says revision is drudgery, I don't agree. You can learn to love tinkering with drafts of poems till a warm hand from somewhere above you reaches down, unscrews the top of your head, and drops in a solution that blows your ears off. Sure, there are plenty of days when nothing good happens, days when every word you write seems silly and shallow, when your revisions seem to be dragging your poems in the wrong direction. But you need to be there writing and waiting, as a hunter might say, for that hour when at last the ducks come flying in. To say it more simply, in the words of a painter friend, you just need to "show up for work."

A couple of years ago, I happened to be talking to a man about pitching horseshoes. He told me his uncle had been a three-state horseshoe champion for several years running. He said he once asked his uncle how he'd gotten so good at the game, and the uncle said, "Son, you got to pitch *a hundred shoes a day*." That's the kind of advice beginning writers should listen to: Keep pitching them horseshoes. We poets serve an art, just as a champion horseshoe pitcher serves his game.

CHAPTER TWO

Writing for Others

While you're working on your poems—writing, revising, maybe starting all over—remind yourself that poetry is communication.

Every teacher of creative writing has at some time had students who resisted all criticism, however constructive and nurturing it might be, and who defended their writing with something like, "It doesn't matter what *you* think of my poem. I just write for *myself!*"

I've tried to persuade those students that the written word was invented to facilitate communication between two or more people, but I've never had much success. On the defensive, they insisted on their right to write for themselves. The poet and teacher Sam Green says he's had students hand him a poem and say, "I wrote this just for myself, but would you mind having a look at it?"

It is, of course, possible to write for one's self, and all of us do it. We jot notes of things to remember, make lists of errands to run, and so on. Your sister, coming upon your scribbled grocery list, understands without a moment's question that what you wrote was not meant for her. Writing that nobody but the author takes interest in—lists of things to pick up at the hardware store, crib sheets for final exams, an address jotted on a napkin—is truly writing for one's self. But poetry is too good a thing to keep to one's self. A poem is meant to be shared with others.

I've inadvertently written lots of poems that meant nothing to anybody else, and I've mailed those poems to editors from coast to coast, hoping that they would be published, only to realize when they were rejected that I'd written them just for myself. I'd been delighted by what I'd written but I hadn't thought enough about the person reading it. For all that my efforts came to I might have saved the postage and humiliation and posted the poems on my refrigerator door like . . . well, grocery lists.

You too will accidentally write poems just for yourself from time to time, spending hours on work that nobody but you has any interest in. When that happens, it may be that you haven't thought enough about the people on the other end of the communication. You choose what to write and how to write it, but if you want to earn an audience for your work, you need to think about the interests, expectations, and needs of others, as well as how you present yourself to them.

THE IMAGINARY READER

I recommend that when you sit down to write you have in mind an imaginary reader, some person you'd like to reach with your words. That person can be anybody, but give it some thought: How old? Level of education? Experience with literature? The more real your imaginary reader seems to you, the easier it becomes to shape a poem that might reach through to that person. If you keep the shadow of that reader—like a whiff of perfume—in the room where you write, you'll be a better writer.

One choice of an imaginary reader is as good as another. Yours might be a chicken plucker in a poultry processing plant or a distinguished professor of choral music. The important thing is to have a sense of the person for whom you are writing and address your work to that person. It needn't be the same imaginary reader for every one of your poems, but with each poem you need to be aware of *somebody* out there who may have occasion to read it. You'll also want to be sure your imaginary reader doesn't shift from one person to another *during the course of a single poem*. For a poem to feel all of a piece, it needs to address a consistent imaginary reader.

The more narrowly you define this reader, the more difficult it will be to put your poem someplace where that reader might come upon it. For example, if your imaginary reader has a PhD in Middle English, you'll have to publish your poem in a journal that might be read by PhDs in Middle English. How many such readers are out there, and how many journals fit that description? On the other hand, if your imaginary reader is somebody with a couple of years of college and an everyday job, there are a lot more readers who fit the description and who may be waiting to discover your poem. The more narrowly you define your reader, the more difficult it becomes for your poem to contact him or her.

In an interesting essay, the critic Sven Birkerts talks about the way in which we read, and how the writer and reader are joined by the experience: "Reading . . . is not simply an inscribing of the author's personal subjectivity upon a reader's receptivity. Rather, it is the collaborative bringing forth of an entire world, a world complete with a meaning structure. For hearing completes itself in listening, and listening happens only where there is some subjective basis for recognition. The work is not merely the bridge between author and reader; it is an enabling entity. The text is a pretext." He then goes on to show how this sense of having a reader serves the writer: "The writer needs the idea of audition—of readers—in order to begin the creative process that gets him beyond the immediate, daily perception of things. In this one sense, the writer does not bring forth the work so much as the work, the idea of it, brings the writer to imaginative readiness."

Keep in mind that most readers of poetry are always slightly on their guard, and your imaginary reader is among them. I've been reading poems for many years and should be altogether comfortable with them, but still, when I turn a page in a literary journal and come upon a poem, I jump back just a little to size up what I'm getting into. Lots of people approach unfamiliar poems with a hollow feeling in their gut because poetry so often presents sizeable challenges for which a reader may be completely unprepared. We've become accustomed to being confronted by poems that confuse, baffle, embarrass, and intimidate us, and for a lot of people, reading poetry is a dreadful experience, that is, an experience full of dread. As poets we need to think about breaking down reader resistance, and having a reader in mind can help.

When I ask you to think about reaching an audience through the help of an imaginary reader, I'm talking about a relatively small audience. If you can develop a handful of devoted readers for your poems, you're doing well. Be realistic about the number of people who read poetry, a tiny portion of the population. Enlisting new readers can be a pretty hard sell. A few new readers of poetry are won over each year, engaged by a poem or two they've happened upon, and that helps to offset the number who give up in despair or out of boredom.

DON'T WEIGH DOWN YOUR POEM WITH SPARE PARTS

When engineers design lawn mowers they don't throw in a lot of extra doodads. Extras in lawn mowers don't help do the work of mowing, and they can make the mower heavier than it ought to be, too hard to push around the yard. And extras can get in the way, can come loose and fall down inside and jam the belt. Extras are also expensive. When it comes to poems, too many extras, too much froufrou and falderal, can cost you a reader.

Have you ever seen one of those illustrated books or articles, drawn from U.S. Patent Office archives, about quaint and curious inventions that never caught on? I remember a drawing of a system of jacks and levers that would tip a man's hat as he approached a woman on the street. I'd guess the inventor thought he had a pretty cool idea. But we all know that unless people see the need to purchase mechanical devices to tip their hats, they won't support an inventor by buying his hat-tipping thingamajigs, no matter how beautifully they are constructed, no matter if they are built as carefully as (dare I say it?) a poem.

There are thousands of writers among us, and each is an inventor. For each invention that catches on with the public—each electric light bulb poem, each jet turbine poem, each "Love Song of J. Alfred Prufrock"— there are hundreds of poems—poems that will automatically tip a gentleman's hat—that fail to engage their readers, primarily because their authors never give their readers' possible needs and interests enough thought. Nobody is going to make use of a mechanical hat-tipping poem for which he doesn't recognize a use.

THE POEM AS A HOUSEGUEST

A poem is the invited guest of its reader. As readers we open the door of the book or magazine, look into the face of the poem, and decide whether or not to invite it into our lives. *No poem has ever entered a reader's life without an invitation; no poem has the power to force the door open. No one is going to read your poem just because it's there.* Because most of our early experience with poems happened in classrooms where we had to try to make sense of a poem, we've gotten the impression that people are going to sit still for a half hour sweating over the poems we write, trying to understand and enjoy them. Not so! In the real world, people know they don't have to understand the hidden meaning of your poem to pass eighth-grade English. They passed eighth-grade English years ago. If your poem doesn't grab them at once, they're turning the page.

Once a poem has been invited in, it can very quickly wear out its welcome. It may tire or offend or bore its hostess and be promptly dismissed. People who read poetry probably dismiss a couple dozen poems for every one they choose to be hospitable toward. The competition is heavy, and there are lots of poems out there waiting for their chance to be invited in. Many that earn invitations will fail to charm or engage their hosts, but a few will succeed, and one or two may be so perfectly suited that they will become a permanent part of their readers' lives, the way Joseph Hutchison's one-line poem describing an artichoke has become part of mine.

The poem I've just described as being successful may sound obsequious, fawning, too eager to please, but I don't mean to leave that impression. You needn't write in words of single syllables. You needn't fall on your knees before your imaginary reader. You needn't pander. You *can* write with difficulty and ambiguity if you envision readers who appreciate difficulty and ambiguity. However you see your imaginary reader, if you write with an abiding sense that *someone* is out there on the other end, someone generous enough to give you a few minutes of their time, you'll make much better choices while you're writing.

I've always liked this very useful passage from John Fowles, author of *The Magus*, *The French Lieutenant's Woman*, and other fine novels. It's from a review of William Trevor's book *The News from Ireland*: "I remember years ago watching the commercial folktale-tellers in a Cairo bazaar. All writers ought to have observed this ancient practice of oral narrative— all critics likewise. Getting the audience, I remarked, depended not at all on preaching and philosophizing but very much on baser tricks of the trade: in short, on pleasing, wooing, luring the listeners into the palm of one's hand."

CHAPTER THREE

First Impressions

The titles and the first few lines of your poem represent the hand you extend in friendship toward your reader. They're the first exposure he or she has, and you want to make a good impression. You also want to swiftly and gracefully draw your reader in.

The poet Leonard Nathan has taught me a great deal during our thirty years' correspondence. If I were to begin a poem like this:

☞✦ A WINTER NIGHT

> It was the 15th of December, snowing
> and I was in Oshkosh, Wisconsin,
> when I . . .

I'd expect Leonard to suggest, "Ted, we don't care whether it was the 15th of the month or the 18th, for one thing, but for another, why don't you put all that exposition (information) into the title? Make it 'A Snowy Night in Oshkosh,' then get on with the poem! We're out here waiting for something to happen."

That exposition should be loaded into titles rather than taking up space in poems is some of the best advice Leonard has given me, and he's given me a lot. He's also a whiz at cutting out unnecessary words. Only rarely have I sent him the draft of a poem in which he didn't find something to prune away.

You can open just about any book of poetry and find poets using titles to carry information. Just look at a table of contents and you'll see how useful titles can be in suggesting what poems will be about. But when choosing a title you have to be careful; titles build expectations. Use a title like "A Snowy Night in Oshkosh" and you'll be expected to follow through with real snow and a real Oshkosh.

You can be creative with titles, using them as the first lines of the poems, where the title works as the first line:

➡ I WALKED INTO THE GREENHOUSE

and picked out a potted plant . . .

Here's one of the most inventive uses of a title I've seen:

➡ AND I RAISED MY HAND IN RETURN

Every morning for two weeks on my walk into the village
I would see the young goat on the grassy slope above the stream.
It belonged to the Gypsies who lived in the plaza below the castle.
One day on my walk back to the mill house I saw the little goat
hanging from a tree by its hind legs, and a Gypsy was pulling
the skin off with a pair of pliers which he waved to me in greeting.

Joseph Stroud's title describes the poet's *response* to the events in the poem itself, suggesting his astonishment when he caught himself raising his hand in greeting, though he might rather have turned away. The title is, in a sense, the conclusion of the poem.

Lots of poets are fond of trumpeting their skill at writing in fixed forms by using the names of those forms in their titles. But if you call your poem "Villanelle on the Opening of the Public Gardens," or "Sonnet on the Falling Leaves," you'd better be pretty good at villanelles or sonnets because, like a gymnast, once you've announced you're going to do three forward flips and a flying cartwheel, everybody in the bleachers is going to expect you to pull it off. With style and grace. If you use a title like "Ghazal to Spring," you need an imaginary reader who knows what a ghazal is. Readers who don't know the literary terms are likely to be irritated; they've only gotten as far as the title and already they feel excluded. I've never seen any advantage in calling attention to the form of the poem. I want *my* imaginary reader to be experiencing the poetry, not drawing back to think about the form and to wonder if Kooser's got all his rhymes in the right places.

In short, a title isn't something you stick on just because you think a poem is supposed to have one. Titles are very important tools for delivering information and setting expectations.

OPENING LINES

If you've ever attended a poetry reading, you know the convention by which the poet introduces his or her poem with a little anecdote: "Well, you know, I wrote this right after I got the news that my house needed to be rewired, which cost a lot, and I just sat down and wrote this little poem about that, so here goes . . ." Then the poet begins reading his poem called "Getting Rewired." It begins, "I had just got the news / that my house needed to be rewired."

But let's say that the really good parts of the poem begin to happen at about the tenth line and all the business about the wiring isn't really all that important. Too often it seems as if, in the poet's first few lines, he or she is writing *toward* the poem, including information that is really not essential but is there because it was a part of the event that triggered the poem. It's the *background story*, and it may not be necessary for us to know it to appreciate the poem.

One evening my wife and I had dinner with an acquaintance who was one of those tedious storytellers who puts every detail into the story just because it happened. If a pencil appears as an incidental detail, we are told that it was a yellow Dixon Ticonderoga about three inches long, with teeth marks and a dried-out pink eraser. Our attention is thus drawn to something that, as it turns out, doesn't much matter. At one point, she mentioned going to a bookstore and kept us waiting a good minute while she tried to remember whether it was Barnes & Noble or Borders. Whether it was one store or the other made no difference whatsoever to the effect of the story, but the teller was intent upon trying to remember which it was, as if remembering that detail were of importance. We sat grinding our teeth until she determined which it had been and went on. No reader will sit still for that kind of dithering in a poem. A poet needs to write with the *essential details. No spare parts.*

Opening lines set up expectations and possibilities. For example, if a poem begins with three lines of strict iambic pentameter, a reader will be disconcerted if that forceful rhythm is abandoned in the fourth line. If you rhyme the first stanza of a poem, the reader will wonder why you didn't rhyme the second and the third.

You can set up the most preposterous event or peculiar situation in the opening couple of lines, like the appearance of a ghost, and there's a very good chance your reader will buy right into it. But you can't wait too long. I'm talking about that business of *the willing suspension of disbelief* that you may remember from literature classes. If you want your readers to suspend disbelief, if you want to put an almond-eyed spaceman in your poem, it's best to get him in there right away.

Let's look at another example, for the matter-of-fact, conversational way in which it opens. The title here establishes the subject, then . . .

•◊ BELLROPE

The line through the hold in the dank
vestibule ceiling ended in
a powerful knot worn slick, swinging
in the breeze from those passing. Half
an hour before service Uncle
Allen pulled the call to worship,
hauling down the rope like the starting
cord of a motor, and the tower
answered and answered, fading
as the clapper lolled aside. I watched
him before Sunday school heave on
the line as on a wellrope. And
the wheel creaked up there as heavy
buckets emptied out their startle
and spread a cold splash to farthest
coves and hollows, then sucked the rope
back into the loft, leaving just
the knot within reach, trembling
with its high connections.

Robert Morgan, who wrote "Bellrope," is one of my favorite contemporary poets. He ushers us into this poem so gracefully and swiftly that we don't quite know how we got comfortably into our pews. By the end of the poem we've been carried into something higher and deeper.

The following poem by R. T. Smith is another good example of how a poet can ease a reader into a poem through unintimidating, conversational language at the beginning. Notice how we are drawn in by what seem to be completely ordinary, everyday statements, and then, how after the poet has made us comfortable he offers us . . . hey! Mozart! From the appearance of the Mozart business the poem begins to lift out and away from the commonplace hardware store toward something bigger. By then we're in our seats, ready for what will happen.

➡◆ HARDWARE SPARROWS

Out for a deadbolt, light bulbs
and two-by-fours, I find a flock
of sparrows safe from hawks

and weather under the roof
of Lowe's amazing discount
store. They skitter from the racks

of stockpiled posts and hoses
to a spill of winter birdseed
on the concrete floor. How

they know to forage here,
I can't guess, but the automatic
door is close enough,

and we've had a week
of storms. They are, after all,
ubiquitous, though poor,

their only song an irritating
noise, and yet they soar
to offer, amid hardware, rope

and handyman brochures,
some relief, as if a flurry
of notes from Mozart swirled

from seed to ceiling, entreating
us to set aside our evening
chores and take grace where

we find it, saying it is possible,
even in this month of flood,
blackout and frustration,

to float once more on sheer
survival and the shadowy
bliss we exist to explore.

OVERLOADING THE OPENING LINES

One caution, though: We can spend so much effort on our opening lines that sometimes they turn out to be the best part of the poem. We polish and polish and polish them until the rest of the poem feels weak by contrast. This is not advisable when it comes to principles of organization, because most good arguments, to use a rhetorical term, build toward strength, toward strong conclusions.

One thing I sometimes try while revising is to turn the poem upside down, to put the last lines first, just to see if that improves it. You may like your poem a little better when it's standing on its head like that. With your original opening lines now at the end of the poem, you'll want to go back and rework the opening lines so that it all seems seamless. Though rewriting may be necessary to make the whole poem flow as one movement, you can often come up with a better poem by just shifting parts of it around. Maybe the ending you've written really belongs in the middle.

THE SPEAKER, OR PRESENCE

The poet's presentation of a speaker is often referred to as *voice*, that voice being the person we not only hear but also intuit to be behind the words. Personality, character, humor, wit, garrulousness, reticence— all those and more can be part of *voice*, or of what I prefer to call *presence*. The presence in and of a poem has a lot to do with the way a reader is affected. For example, a presence with personal charm is a lot more likely to engage a reader than a presence who sneers at its audience, or who seems mean or arrogant or self-pitying.

I've included my ideas about presence in the same chapter with my thoughts on titles and openings because a reader starts seeking a presence at once, trying to get a sense of the speaker during the first words he or she reads.

The presence in a poem can be the poet or a speaker whom the poet creates, a *persona*. Presence is the sum of what a reader learns about the poem's speaker's experience, character, feelings, and manner of address from what is written. Some poems tell us very little about the person behind the words, and concentrate instead on what is seen in the world beyond that speaker's point of view. Other poems tell us very little about the world and tell us a great deal about the person portrayed by the words.

Presence is revealed not only through what is said, which is substance, but also by how it is said, which is style. Since every poem has a presence, think about the idea of presence while you're reading the poems of others. You'll teach yourself some valuable things. And as you write your poems, think about the kind of presence you're projecting.

AT A WINDOW ON THE WORLD

Here's a way of thinking about the degree of your own presence in a poem: How much do we learn about you, or the first-person speaker?

While choosing your words it is as if you were at a window looking out into the world. If the light that falls upon what lies beyond is very bright, you see the scene in vivid colors and there is only the faintest hint of your reflection in the glass. If the light beyond the window is faint, as at dusk, the speaker's reflection in the glass is much more prominent. The speaker notices both his or her reflection and the scene beyond. And if it has grown dark outside, dark enough to make a mirror of the window, the speaker, or presence, sees very little other than his or her own reflection. In such a poem, presence is pronounced and superior to what is outside.

The poem is the record of a moment at that window, but for once the author—not time nor weather—gets to control the amount of light outside. For once, you are in charge of the sun. If you want to write a poem about yourself, you turn down the light on the world and thus brighten your reflection in the glass. If you don't want to appear very prominently in your poem you brighten the light on the world until your reflection all but disappears. But there is always this double image, made up of the poet's reflection in the glass—perhaps vivid, perhaps faint, perhaps somewhere in between—as well as what is in the world beyond, which is also to some degree vivid or faint.

Though I said earlier that I intend to use contemporary poems as examples, this poem by Emily Dickinson is useful. It's a work in which the poet's reflection in the glass is vivid, and the objective world beyond has been darkened:

> It's all I have to bring today—
> This, and my heart beside—
> This, and my heart, and all the fields—
> And all the meadows wide—
> Be sure you count—should I forget
> Some one the sum could tell—
> This, and my heart, and all the Bees
> Which in the Clover dwell.

There is nothing in this poem that suggests the poet is looking beyond herself. She's looking at her reflection. Sure, there are mentions of fields and meadows, but we know she's not really looking at them. The poem is all in her head.

Here, on the other hand, is a poem by Brewster Ghiselin, written in the mid–twentieth century. In it the light is bright beyond the window and the poet's reflection is limited to the use, here and there, of the personal pronoun *I*.

◦◦ RATTLESNAKE

> I found him sleepy in the heat
> And dust of a gopher burrow,
> Coiled in loose folds upon silence
> In a pit of the noonday hillside.
> I saw the wedged bulge
> Of the head hard as a fist.
> I remembered his delicate ways:
> The mouth a cat's mouth yawning.
> I crushed him deep in dust,
> And heard the loud seethe of life
> In the dead beads of the tail
> Fade, as wind fades
> From the wild grain of the hill.

Poets are usually quite consistent in the amount of light they put on the world beyond the glass, poem after poem. There are poets like Ghiselin, whose life work gives us the world outside with such vividness that we scarcely see his reflection, and poets like Dickinson, who darkens the light on the world enough to keep her reflections always before us. Sometimes poets gradually change during a long life of writing, moving away from fixing a bright light on the world beyond them toward more and more revelation of their personalities. I've done that myself. Or they may move in the opposite direction, beginning their writing careers with poems about themselves but gradually become more and more devoted to portraying the world beyond them.

No matter how a poet sets up the double image, the resulting poem must engage a reader or it fails. With Dickinson's poem, the voice we hear as we read the words—its personality, its wit, its charm—is the principal engaging force. With a poem like Ghiselin's, we are engaged by the vivid picture Ghiselin summons up through his use of imagery. Readers can also be engaged by the music of a poem, its rhythms, its combinations of sounds, the feeling in their throats as they sound out the words. There's nothing wrong with a poet having fun.

Successful poems often take advantage of several approaches, mixing the personal revelation of a poem like Dickinson's with the objective observation of a poem like Ghiselin's.

No matter how you write, poorly or well, a reader will sense a presence. It's your job as you revise to think about the presence you're communicating. What will your reader think of the person who comes through the words, and how can your reader's assessment be directed and controlled? A great part of the poem's effect on its reader has to do with presence.

While writing and revising, think about the presence you're projecting. Also, do as much as you can with your titles and opening lines, keeping in mind your imaginary reader. Give those titles and openings a cost-benefit analysis: How much do you gain by using the beginning you've written, versus how much might it cost you by putting off your reader? Think of how wary he or she may be when entering the drafty walkway up to the waiting plane of your poem. Like a good flight assistant, you may want to get your readers belted into their seats before you start telling them that the weather ahead is expected to be turbulent.

And while you're reading poetry, study the ways in which your favorite poems open. How much have their authors asked of you as their reader, and how hard have they worked to graciously invite you in?

CHAPTER FOUR

Don't Worry about the Rules

Beginning poets often ask first about rules: Do you always have to capitalize the first word in every line? And so on. Well, there are no *shoulds* or *should nots* in writing poetry. You can do whatever you feel like doing, pants on or pants off. Part of the joy of writing, or of practicing any art, comes from the freedom to choose.

When Cezanne painted a landscape, he chose not to render it photographically even though he had the skill to do so. The hills and forests that lay in the distance were merely a convenient structure upon which he could arrange his paint—believing, I'd guess, that a painting is about the application of pigment to a surface and not solely about representing subject matter. One of the great discoveries of modern art was that paintings could be objects, that they didn't need to be *pictures*. Cezanne felt free to make the choice not to represent those hills exactly but rather with expression. If there were Art Cops saying painters shouldn't be doing that, well, he did it anyway. And when writing poetry, whether to write a sonnet or a villanelle or an open form poem is the uninhibited choice of its author. You have the freedom to use whichever tools best serve your poetry.

We're accustomed to rules for just about everything we do, from wearing a hairnet in a restaurant kitchen to the proper way to make pan gravy, heating the grease to the right temperature and then very carefully folding in the flour with a fork, so it's reasonable that we would expect to have rules set for us when we write poetry. But no matter what you've been told, a haiku does not have to have seventeen syllables and, though a sonnet is supposed to be written in fourteen lines of iambic pentameter with a specific pattern of rhymes, it doesn't have to go *da-dum, da-dum, da-dum,* all the way through, beating the gongs of perfect rhymes, *love/dove, sweet/feet.*

Here, for example, is a contemporary sonnet by Kim Addonizio:

●◆ AQUARIUM

> The fish are drifting calmly in their tank
> between the green reeds, lit by a white glow
> that passes for the sun. Blindly, the blank
> glass that holds them in displays their slow
> progress from end to end, familiar rocks
> set into the gravel, murmuring rows
> of filters, a universe the flying fox
> and glass cats, Congo tetras, bristle-nosed
> plecostemus all take for granted. Yet
> the platys, gold and red, persist in leaping
> occasionally, as if they can't quite let
> alone a possibility—of wings,
> maybe, once they reach the air? They die
> on the rug. We find them there, eyes open in surprise.

Notice how the regular iambic pentameter of line one:

> The FISH are DRIFTing CALMly IN their TANK

is varied in line 2 to accommodate the natural cadence of conversation:

> betwEEN the GREEN REEDS, LIT by a WHITE GLOW

Then, so as to hang onto and preserve the rhythm of the basic under-structure, the poet returns to the regular iambic rhythm in line three, reversing one foot, the fourth:

> that PASSES FOR the SUN. BLINDly, the BLANK

She could have written something like:

> that PASSES FOR the SUN. So BLIND, the BLANK

but that wouldn't have sounded natural, would it? She wants this poem to sound like something that somebody living today would say. She doesn't want it to sound as if somebody in the 1600s were saying it.

And, of course, where true rhymes like *tank/blank* and *glow/slow* fall naturally into place, she doesn't hesitate to get away from perfect rhymes when the language feels more conversational without them: *leaping/wings, die/surprise.*

If more poems were written like this, to mimic real contemporary speech, there'd be a bigger audience for poetry. Kim Addonizio has a sizeable following for her work, partly because her work is broadly accessible, or so I see it.

For *The Poetry Home Repair Manual*, which has no aspirations to be a manual of forms, one close look at a sonnet like Addonizio's ought to be enough. There are dozens of excellent books about poetic forms, giving you all sorts of examples, and I don't intend for this book to enter that competition. A couple of reasonably priced and useful books are Alfred Corn's *The Poem's Heartbeat: A Manual of Prosody* (Story Line Press, 1997) and Steve Kowit's *In the Palm of Your Hand: The Poet's Portable Workshop* (Tilbury House, 1995). If you are fond of owning a shelf of fat reference books, you might pick up (being sure to lift with your knees!) the 1,383-page *Princeton Encyclopedia of Poetry and Poetics* (MJF Books, 1993). Purchase one of the many manuals, study it, and experiment for fun and exercise with writing lines in meter, and with writing sonnets and ballads and villanelles and so forth, keeping in mind that what you are writing are not poems but *exercises*, like doing pull-ups. You've got a better chance of winning the lottery than of writing a good poem the first time you try a pantoum (I'll let you look that one up). And no person has written poetry just because he or she has dutifully filled out the rhyme scheme of a Petrarchan sonnet.

But of course it can be fun to write in fixed forms, and perhaps you'll be one of those poets who can excel within the rules and limitations. If you want to see just one example of how well and with what grace a contemporary poet can write in fixed forms, take a look at Richard Wilbur's *New and Collected Poems* (Harcourt Brace Jovanovich, 1998).

Having excused myself from talking at length about forms, I do want to mention a few things about the mechanics of poetry that may be helpful.

Let's take a step back and return to the subject of communication, and to my idea that writing poetry is a way in which one person reaches out to another. Whether you choose fixed or free form, you make that choice to make your communication more effective.

In daily life, when you want to get your Aunt Jerusha to do something, you know how to go about it. You know what's likely to keep her interested, and you know how to organize what you say so you can be pretty sure she'll respond in the way you expect. Or maybe you're not trying to make her take action; maybe you're only trying to get her to look at things your way. Whatever the circumstances, you can think of writing your poem as a means of persuasion because a poem can be looked at as something designed *to bring about an action*. That action need not be more than a momentary change of mood, or a realization. Let your instincts about how human beings relate to one another be a guide to how you write. Whatever you learn as you write, you need to keep in mind that, in spite of the form you choose—be it sonnet or free form—you have the opportunity to be accommodating and hospitable toward your readers, as is Kim Addonizio's sonnet on the aquarium.

One of my teachers who loved rules once said to me, "In a line of iambic pentameter, it is permissible to substitute a trochee or spondee or anapest or dactyl for an iamb, but only in the first or third foot, never in the second or fourth." Well, how can anybody write well with restrictions like that?

John Berger, the English novelist and critic, says in one of his essays about painting that *in the work of a master the form seems inevitable*, and if you look at successful poems you can see how right Berger is. *Every successful sonnet is a good poem first and a good sonnet second*. The poetry must lead and the form follow, if only a heartbeat behind. Or we might say that the poetry and the form must be perfectly integrated.

Thousands of readers love Robert Frost's "Stopping by Woods on a Snowy Evening," but very few of us care that it was written in a complicated form with a demanding rhyme scheme. The beauty of Frost's poetry catches the reader, not the fact that he was able to shoehorn that beauty into a difficult literary structure. Of course, the form lends rhythm and music, but we don't start out by remarking upon the form. Surely Frost must have been pleased with himself for mastering that structure, for meeting its difficult challenges, but just as surely he would have known that the great majority of his readers would probably appreciate his poem without noticing this technical accomplishment, being, as could be expected, far more engaged by the poem's atmospheric effects: the little horse with its harness bells, the mysterious wood, and the soft and silent snow. The complicated literary form of "Stopping by Woods" is inseparable from the poem, of course, but it is all but invisible to the average reader. One of that poem's most important achievements is to have kept its structure from calling attention to itself.

When it comes to the form your poem takes, you can determine it *as* you write. "Every force evolves a form," said the Shakers, who built beautiful yet functional furniture and tools. As you work on your poem, try to see what shape the poetry wants to assume. Do the lines feel best when they're short or long? When you say the poem aloud, or ask a friend to read it back to you, are there places at which you can't take a breath? And so on. In that way, you can help make sure that the poem's form feels natural. As you revise, with care, *your poem will develop toward the form it ought to have.* You almost always hurt a poem if you choose its structure before you concentrate on giving shape to an experience or emotion. It is the *process* of writing that urges the writer toward a poem's most natural, most effective form. The decisions are best made en route. I may be wrong, but I'd be willing to bet that Kim Addonizio didn't sit down to write a sonnet, but rather to write about the fish in the aquarium. As her poem began to shape itself, she discovered that a few rhymes were falling into place and the poem seemed to be leaning toward becoming a sonnet and that it might work most effectively *as* a sonnet. I'd guess she made a few small alterations, tipping it toward the sonnet form, and there it was.

Every successful poem is unique and personal. It abides by its *own* rules of order. It has form, no matter whether its words are scattered randomly or stacked in neat lines, each with a uniform number of stresses. It has form because its maker arrived at a decision about placing each word, each punctuation mark, each phrase, and each rhythmical device in accordance with a personal standard of perfection. That standard of perfection is the organizing principle that determines a poem's form.

If you'd like proof of the presence of this kind of organic form, even in a poem that looks like "free verse," just suggest to the poet that she change the order of words in a phrase. You'll likely meet with fierce resistance because her choice of those words—and every word of the poem—were an integral part of the poem's organization. To a poet each word is like a gear in a clock. To make the clock keep time with an alternative part, you'd have to find a gear with the same diameter and same number of teeth. Dropping a synonym into a poem's clockworks, for example, can be wrong because of the synonym's sound, its combination of consonants and vowels, or because of the pattern in which its syllables receive emphasis, or because it ever so slightly differs in meaning from the original word.

But I do want to emphasize that self-education in the mechanics of fixed forms, and of the effects of rhyme and meter, can be very helpful. Rhyme and meter and the other identifiable devices used in poetry are basic tools, like hammers and saws, and the more tools you have at hand to select from, the better you're likely to write.

For example, knowing how meter can speed up or slow down the reader can add effective emphasis to what the poet wishes to say. In Karl Shapiro's poem "Mongolian Idiot," he writes:

> At thirty-five he squeals to see the ball
> Bounce in the air and roll away.

The pattern of accented syllables in those lines is:

> at THIRty-FIVE he SQUEALS to SEE the BALL
> BOUNCE in the AIR and ROLL aWAY.

Notice how the pattern *ta* DUM, *ta* DUM, *ta* DUM, *ta* DUM, *ta* DUM of the first line is artfully changed to DUM *ta da* DUM at the beginning of the second line, emphasizing the word *bounce*. By altering the rhythm, Shapiro gives the ball a little extra bounce. No one told Karl Shapiro in advance of his writing "Mongolian Idiot" that there was a rule for all Down syndrome poems that stated he must always reverse the rhythm in the first foot of line eighteen. Instead, Shapiro's choice was made during the *process* of writing, when he came to those lines and determined to take advantage of an opportunity to strengthen their effect by using the tool of metrical substitution.

Another masterful example of using rhythm to suggest movement is the opening sentence of Richard Wilbur's "Juggler":

> A ball will bounce, but less and less.

There are innumerable examples of lines with sounds that suggest the motion of something being described, such as "I galloped, Dirk galloped, we galloped all three," and each of you can probably recall some teacher telling you to look for them. I here join the ranks of those moldy professors, chalk dust all over their vests, emphatically tapping their blackboards: You can learn a lot from looking closely at the small effects as well as the big ones.

As an example of the deft use of rhythm, I want to say something about two interesting lines in a poem by the eleventh-century Chinese poet Su Tung-p'o. I like Su Tung-p'o for his remarkable clarity, freshness, and candor, which have helped his poems survive nearly a thousand years. He lived a rich but troubled life and wrote about almost everything that happened to him, small and large, with good humor and humility.

The credit for the following rhythmic accomplishments goes of course to Burton Watson, the translator:

> Long rapids drop steeply, waves leap up;
> the light boat shoots south like a plunging shuttle.

Notice how in that first phrase there is a dropping rhythm: LONG RAPids DROP STEEPly, followed immediately by the phrase WAVES LEAP UP, which suggests the waves leaping. But the second line is even more masterful, with the string of accents, LIGHT BOAT SHOOTS SOUTH suggesting the driving action of the boat. And then there follows the wonderfully subtle

> like a PLUNGing SHUTtle

which by its pattern of accents mirrors the action of a shuttle, weaving in and out of the threads of a loom. This is the work of a true master of rhythm.

Poets who have the ability to hear their words as they write them, to feel the words in their throats, quite often write this way without thinking much about it. We can't know whether Burton Watson labored to write these lines in just this way or whether they came to him without effort. If as a young person you learned to read without sounding out the words in your head, to take the symbol of the word directly into your mind as a meaning, you are at a slight disadvantage as a poet, but you can counter that by reading your drafts aloud to yourself, which will immediately make you aware of the sounds and rhythms you've put into your work.

As a poet you need to be aware that rhythm in language can effectively suggest the rhythm of an action described, but it would be discouraging, if not paralyzing, if you slowed yourself almost to a standstill just to work on an effect. You can easily lose the driving impulse behind your poem by stopping to get analytical. It is usually far better to push on to the end, riding the wave of your inspiration. Then later, during revision, you can go over what you've written and see what can be achieved by making adjustments here and there.

There are a number of ways of creating rhythms with words on paper. The manuals I mentioned earlier are useful in understanding these variations.

Let's look at this poem:

⇢ THE MEN WHO RAISED THE DEAD

If they had hair it was gray,
the backs of their hands wormy
currents of blue veins, old men
the undertaker believed
had already lost too much
to the earth to be bothered
by what they found, didn't find,
brought there that May afternoon
dogwood trees bloomed like white wreaths
across Jocassee's valley.

They took their time, sought the shade
when they tired, let cigarettes
and silence fill the minutes

until the undertaker
nodded at his watch, and they
worked again, the only sound
the rasp and shuck of shovels
as they settled deeper in graves
twice-dug, sounding for the thud
of struck wood not always found—
sometimes something other, silk
scarf or tie, buckle, button,
nestled in some darker earth,
enough to give a name to.

One quit before they were done,
lay down as if death were now
too close to resist, and so
another stepped in his grave,
finished up, but not before
they shut his eyes, laid him with
all the others to be saved
if not from death, from water.

This poem by Ron Rash is written in syllabics. Syllabic measure is
quite popular today because it has an easygoing, conversational feeling
to it. Syllabic measure sets line length by counting the number of
syllables. This differs from accentual measure, which counts only the
number of accents per line, and from traditional meters like blank verse
(unrhymed iambic pentameter), which tries for a consistent number of
both accented and unaccented syllables, with occasional variances.

Reading Rash's poem, it's unlikely that you would have noticed its
form had I not called your attention to it. The poem looks and sounds
like "free verse," but it isn't "free" at all. Count the number of syllables
in each line and you'll be surprised at how meticulously the poem is
kept to seven syllables per line. I know Rash's poetry quite well, and
this seems to be his favorite form. I have one of his books in which
nearly every poem is like this, seven syllables per line, but his counting
is handled so deftly that most readers would never notice it.

Syllabic form doesn't in any way require or demand that you count out *every* line as you write it, but it does provide a means of keeping the flow of the poem under some control and helps to establish an underlying and unobtrusive rhythmical shape that the reader may feel even though it remains hidden. The way our language works, if you confine a line to seven syllables, you'll average maybe three hard accents per line, so in a sense you are also setting up a measure of accents, too.

You might wonder why a poet like Rash would so rigidly confine himself to seven syllables, and I can't answer for him, but I do know that any time you are writing in a form, you are writing up against its walls, and sometimes you are forced by those walls to fall back and say things in a fresh new way. Writing in form causes you to twist your words this way and that to make them fit the pattern, and surprising things can happen, even lucky things. Sure, Rash is following a rule, but it's his own rule, not somebody else's. If he put eight syllables in one of his lines, and it felt right that way, nobody would care, the Poetry Cops wouldn't break down the door of his study and read him his rights. His choice to use seven syllables per line is an example of one poet's freedom to write as he wishes.

CHAPTER FIVE

Rhyming, Ham Cubes,
Prose Poems

Poems don't have to rhyme, but rhyming can add to the pleasure of reading. It can also help if you want to recite a poem from memory because rhyme and meter are mnemonic devices, that is, they assist us in memorizing. For most of us, poems written in free form are more difficult to remember.

There are thousands of good examples of rhyme, and if you've ever studied poetry in a classroom you've no doubt been taught about rhyme schemes, that is, patterns of end rhymes, in sonnets, in couplets, and so on. Again, any good manual on verse will have everything you ever wanted to know about rhyming.

The following poem is a very good example of effective, *unobtrusive* rhyming of a different sort.

⚭ SEA HORSE

You might think it would leap the waves
in a white fire of foam
racing, eyes mad with what might
be delight:

a runaway, or loosed from a god's
team, galloping in its vast
pasture. But this one
was the size of a brooch, thin, and red-gold, and still.

The children had sent for it
from the Atlantic.
It arrived by air in a pouch of seawater containing
all it needed to sustain life as it crossed the continent.

Following instructions
we made it a small, nourishing ocean
in which it anchored itself upright
to a strand of seaweed, and, staring jewel-eyed

at nothing, slowly faded white
and died.

My guess is that on first reading of this poem by Edward Weismiller
you may not have noticed any rhymes at all, or at most just a few.
But on close examination there are lots of rhymes here, nestled inside
conversational language, and lending the poem a little subtle music.
Below, I've capitalized some of the true rhymes:

You MIGHT think it would leap the waves
in a WHITE fire of foam
racing, eyes mad with what MIGHT
be DELIGHT:

a runaway, or loosed from a god's
team, galloping in its VAST
PASture. But this one
was the size of a brooch, thin, and red-gold, and still.

The children had sent for it
from the Atlantic.
It arrived by air in a pouch of seawater CONTAINing
all it needed to SUSTAIN life as it crossed the continent.

Following instructions
we made it a small, nourishing ocean
in which it anchored itself upRIGHT
to a strand of seaweed, and, staring jewel-EYED

at nothing, slowly faded WHITE
and DIED.

Then, of course, there are subtle slant or partial rhymes, like in-
strucTIONS/OCEANS.

Because so many of the true rhymes fall in the middle of phrases,
we breeze over them quickly. Internal rhymes are less prominent than

end rhymes. Weismiller uses hard end rhymes in the last four lines, for example, when he wants to seal up the poem as if with a few stomps of his foot. Before that, the rhymes are softer, less likely to call attention to themselves.

Graceful, unobtrusive rhyming can add a great deal to the effect of a poem written in rather plain language. What might at first glance appear to be a mere conversational anecdote about a sea horse is dignified, enhanced, and made musical by the poet's carefully handled rhymes and his excellent sense of pacing.

An aside: Notice also how Weismiller plays with slightly inflated literary language in the opening six-and-a-half lines and then shifts into a plainer style when he wants to convey the smallness and ordinariness of this little death. The contrast is quite effective in making the sea horse seem diminutive.

Of course, when it comes to the "music" of a poem, in addition to rhyme, you have at your disposal the tools of alliteration, assonance, consonance, and so on. I don't intend to define those here. Any good dictionary can explain them in a phrase or two.

FIXED FORMS AND HAM CUBES

The butchers at the Pac 'N' Save where I shop have started using equipment that form-fits a plastic covering over the ham cubes they sell for making ham and bean soup, one of my favorite winter meals. The ham cubes lie in the open refrigerated counters looking just like loose piles of ham chunks upon which is a shiny, see-through coating. I suppose it's a kind of shrink-wrap, done with heavier plastic. It used to be that I would buy a little Styrofoam tray of ham cubes with a sheet of plastic wrap stretched over it. Quite a bit of empty grocery store air got sealed in the tray with the ham. But with the new equipment there's scarcely a bubble of space that isn't taken up by pure ham. Maybe you too have seen meat packaged this way.

The form of a poem ought to be like that. What's important, after all, is the ham cubes—that is, the words and images of the poem, not what contains them. The form ought to fit the poem just like that shrink-wrap, and be just that transparent, so you can look right through the form to the ham.

When you're trying to write in fixed form, writing sonnets and sestinas and pantoums and who knows what, you're getting out Styrofoam trays and filling them with ham cubes. The sonnet is the tray and the poem is the ham. All too often the tray is in charge of how the poem winds up looking. A villanelle tray or a sestina tray will hold just so much ham, and if you don't put enough meat in, the poem looks like there's too much air in the package. It just doesn't have that sleek, shrink-wrapped feeling that you get when the form seems to extend from the meat itself. And if you put in more ham than the little tray can handle, the poem bulges and looks like it might pop open in your bag before you get it home. Writing poems in fixed forms can be difficult because you have to carefully count and sort and place the ham cubes till they fit precisely into the tray. When it works, you've got something that looks just fine and doesn't call too much attention to itself. Your reader says, "Oh, look, ham cubes. I'd better get some for the soup."

If you want to try writing in fixed forms, that's how you do it well: Not one ham cube too many, not one too few. You can see the shrink-wrap and the tray, of course, but never do they get in the way of displaying the poetry. Form is an integral part of any art because art affirms order, but the form you choose doesn't have to be somebody else's form. It can be yours; and, as in Ron Rash's poem in syllabics, "The Men Who Raised the Dead," cited in the last chapter, it can even be kept hidden.

Here's a poem by B. H. Fairchild in fixed form, a sestina, into which the poetry fits comfortably:

◗◆ THERE IS CONSTANT MOVEMENT IN MY HEAD

The choreographer from Nebraska
is listening to her mother's cane
hammering the dance floor, down down,
like some gaunt, rapacious bird
digging at a rotted limb. The mother
still beats time in her daughter's head.

There is constant movement in my head,
the choreographer begins. In Nebraska
I learned dance and guilt from my mother,
held my hands out straight until the cane

beat my palms blue. I was a wild bird
crashing into walls, calming down

only to dance. When Tallchief came down
from New York, a dream flew into my head:
to be six feet tall, to dance the Firebird
all in black and red, to shock Nebraska
with my naked, crazy leaps until the cane
shook in the furious hand of my mother.

Well, that day never came. My mother
thought I could be whittled down,
an oak stump to carve into some cane
she could lean on. But in my head
were the sandhill cranes that crossed Nebraska
each fall: sluggish, great-winged birds

lumbering from our pond, the air bird—
heavy with cries and thrumming. My mother
knew. She said I would leave Nebraska,
that small-town life could only pull me down.
Then her hands flew up around her head
and she hacked at the air with her cane.

There are movements I can't forget: the cane
banging the floor, dancers like huge birds
struggling into flight, and overhead,
the choreography of silver cranes my mother
always watched when the wind blew down
from the sandhills and leaves fell on Nebraska.

This dance is the cane of my mother.
The dancers are birds that will never come down.
They were all in my head when I left Nebraska.

A sestina requires the use of the same six end words in a specific
pattern of repetition. Writing a sestina is a whole hell of a lot of work,
but some poets like the challenge of seeing if they can write one that
turns out to be poetry and not just evidence of heavy lifting. All too

often the form takes over completely and the language gets all bent out of shape, which is one of the persistent problems of working in any fixed form, but Fairchild does a good job of making an effective poem using this difficult, rule-ridden form.

Note his choice of end words. When writing a sestina it is easiest to pick rather common end words, words that one might possibly repeat in conversation. Just for kicks, awhile back I wrote the following example, trying to mimic the recorded voice you hear in interstate highway rest stop restrooms, that monotone voice that drones on and on 24/7 about the weather, informing the empty toilet stalls and the mud-smeared floor which roads are safe. I wanted to convey how very dull and dead is that voice, but also how very tedious the sestina form can be:

➡◇ WEATHER SESTINA

Statewide sleet and rain this morning, worse
by mid day, with flurries predicted west
of a line from Rushville to Oshkosh, spreading east
by nightfall. Considerably colder in the north
tonight, lows in the teens, but warmer south,
up into the thirties. If you have to travel, better

check with the State Patrol for conditions. Better
be safe than sorry. It's going to get worse
with possibly treacherous roads in the south
because of the warmer temperatures. In the west,
increasing to heavy snow by midnight. North,
colder with snow and blowing snow. East

of a line from North Platte north and all of east-
ern Nebraska, winter snow warning, no better
by morning and possibly colder, with north-
erly winds and drifting making the roads worse
statewide. Snow and ice-packed highways west,
snow and slush with possible heavy icing south.

Travelers in Kansas will want to keep south
of a line from Colby to Leavenworth. East

of Manhattan, rain and freezing rain, but west
of a line from Liberal to Atwood, better
with gradual clearing and nothing much worse
than snow and some light icing north.

Back to Nebraska. Tonight, in the north,
expect heavy accumulations. In the south,
four to six inches of new snow, worse
toward the Colorado border. In the east
tonight, snow and blowing snow, no better
by morning. Then gradual clearing west

of a line from Kimball to Scottsbluff. West-
ern Nebraska, clearing but colder with north
to northwesterly winds, with the roads no better
because of the drifting. Then clearing south
with slowly improving road conditions east
of a line from Hebron to Fordyce, worse

roads to the west, best roads to the south.
You folks in the north and in the east
stay off the roads. You're in this for better or worse.

Yes, that's the voice a man might hear as he looks down at the blue
sanitary tablet floating over the drain in the urinal. This sestina was
originally published in a literary magazine, probably because it's a
spoof of sestinas, rather than because it's a good poem. The editor
didn't tell me why he took it.

PROSE POEMS

I've talked a little about traditional forms of versification, but you may
be interested in writing what are called "prose poems." Let me say a
few things about these before we get away from thoughts about form
and into other matters.

What is a prose poem?

Let's start by looking at prose nonfiction as a continuum, with all of
the possible variations blending or blurring one into another. Across
this continuum play two shifting strains, the emphasis upon truth and
the revelation of the speaker's personality.

On one end is the technical article, a clearly written, factual piece instructing a person in how to install a memory chip or use a new food processor. In the standard technical article there is no sense of an individual speaking. If a personality were to show through the writing, the article would feel peculiar to us, even off-putting. When we go to a technical article we are simply looking for instruction and we have no interest in making the acquaintance of the author. The craft in technical writing is to reach the highest standards of clarity and accessibility while suppressing personality.

Next to the technical article, across a blurry border, is what we loosely call journalism. Journalism varies in its revelations about the author. Daily news reporting requires the suppression of the writer's personality while feature writing includes more of a sense of his or her interests and motives. Columnists like Molly Ivins become well known to us through their revelations about themselves. What we like or dislike about them comes from our opinion of what they say as well as how we feel about them as people. In the opinion column, as in the technical article, the craft is in writing clearly and accessibly, though feature and opinion writing and sometimes daily news writing may incorporate literary devices such as figurative language.

Next to journalism, and just across the border from the opinion column, is the personal essay or personal narrative, in which a speaker tells us a great deal about himself or herself, often through direct, first-person revelation. Generally speaking, the craft of the personal essay can be difficult to distinguish from the craft of personal journalism, but we tend to think of the successful essay as having a longer half-life than personal journalism, since journalism, as the *jour* part its name suggests, is about things of the moment, or ephemera, while we expect essays to be more farsighted and less tied to topical occurrences. But again, this is a very blurry area, and personal essays sometimes appear in newspapers just as personal journalism sometimes appears in collections of essays.

Though writers of good personal essays and journalism sometimes employ literary devices—figurative language, rhythm, pacing—to enhance effects, the authors of prose poems make even more use of those tools, exercising very selective care in all aspects of writing, from word choice and word order to speech rhythms and the play of the sound of syllables upon each other. In a personal essay it might be possible to change a word or two without much diminishing the overall effect, but changing a single word in a prose poem (or any form of poetry) can damage it to a considerable degree.

Prose poems require the same amount of care that lined verse requires, but the writer of a prose poem forgoes the tool of line endings, and a line ending is a powerful tool. That open space out there at the end of a line of verse is a kind of punctuation. It can control the manner in which the reader is drawn through the poem. Even though the prose poem author puts aside this important tool, he or she gains another tool, which is to take advantage of the ease and confidence with which a reader approaches prose as opposed to poetry. Lots of readers are intimidated by the appearance of poetry, saying to themselves as they come upon a poem, as if they were about to step on a snake, "Uh-oh! It's a poem! LOOK OUT!" On the other hand, we are all so accustomed to the appearance of prose that we enter a prose poem without much fear.

Here's a very good example of a prose poem, by Robert Bly:

❧ LOOKING AT A DEAD WREN IN MY HAND

Forgive the hours spent listening to radios, and the words of gratitude I did not say to teachers. I love your tiny rice-like legs, that are bars of music played in an empty church, and the feminine tail, where no worms of Empire have ever slept, and the intense yellow chest that makes tears come. Your tail feathers open like a picket fence, and your bill is brown, with the sorrow of an old Jew whose daughter has married an athlete. The black spot on your head is your own mourning cap.

I've mentioned elsewhere that during the process of writing, a poem may seek its own form, and sometimes a poem that begins as lined-out verse might wind up as a prose poem, or vice versa. The quality of the poetry always counts for more than does the satisfaction of a literary shape.

This chapter and the previous one have scarcely touched on the complex study of prosody, a word I've intentionally avoided above because it sounds so stuffy, but which is in fact the proper term for the science of poetic forms. Science is OK, but as you know, *heart* is better. Here's something to reflect upon from Trepliov's last speech in Chekhov's *The Sea Gull*: "I'm coming more and more to the conclusion that it's a matter not of old forms and not of new forms, but that a man writes, not thinking at all of what form to choose, writes because it comes pouring out from his soul."

I urge you to write from your soul no matter what form you choose because that's what really matters. You want to write poems that connect with others, that can show your readers new ways of seeing, understanding, and enjoying the world. Again, you can define those readers however you wish. But whether you are hoping to reach one very special reader or a broad general audience, write from the heart and let your poems find their shapes (forms) as you proceed, then perfect what you've written through careful revision.

CHAPTER SIX

Writing about Feelings

Poetry would be a lost art if there were laws against writing about feelings, and the Poetry Cops would be very busy pounding on poets with night sticks.

In response to great loss, like the terrorist attacks on the World Trade Center and the Pentagon, people all over the country sat down to write poems. Thousands of poems were written opposing our country's war on Iraq. Most of these well-meaning poems fail as art, but they do make their writers feel better, because we all feel better for having expressed ourselves and because people understand that a poem is a way of assembling a little bit of order amid chaos.

To write a poem that is not just a gush of sentiment but something that will engender in its readers deep, resonant feelings, you need to exercise restraint to avoid what is commonly termed sentimentality.

Sentimentality is defined by the dictionaries as "an excess of sentiment," or "the affectation of sentiment," but those definitions beg for further definitions of "excess" and "affectation" and "sentiment." If you begin to follow this branching trail you'll soon discover that there is a whole lot of confusion when it comes to defining sentimentality.

If you look up sentimentality in a guidebook on writing, it's likely you'll find one of those dictionary definitions followed by what the author considers to be a good example. Even if the example seems obvious, gushy, and mawkish, you can be certain a few readers will stare at it and say to themselves, "Well, that's not really all that bad, is it?"

Edgar Guest, a popular poet of the early twentieth century, wrote this poem:

Never a sigh for the cares that she bore for me,
Never a thought of the joys that flew by;
Her one regret that she couldn't do more for me,
Thoughtless and selfish, her master was I.

Oh, the long nights that she came at my call to me!
Oh, the soft touch of her hands on my brow!
Oh, the long years that she gave up her all to me!
Oh, how I yearn for her gentleness now!

Slave to her baby! Yes, that was the way of her,
Counting her greatest of services small;
Words cannot tell what this old heart would say of her,
Mother—the sweetest and fairest of all.

I showed this poem to my friend, the poet Bob King, and he felt that its greatest sins are generalizations: the joys, the long years, greatest of services, gentleness, and so on. He's correct in suggesting that by using generalizations like "the good old days," a writer might hope to touch some sentimental heartstrings. But think of how much more effective Guest's poem would have been if he had shown his mother performing some *specific* act of caring, maybe bringing a cup of tea with honey to the bedside during a bout of strep throat.

Leonard Nathan gave me a pretty useful definition of sentimentality. He said it is "a kind of disproportion between excessive feeling and its object." An example might be a poem in which an excess of emotion is lavished on a floor lamp.

Whatever the definition we prefer, sentimentality is entirely in the eye of the beholder. People who keep their emotions under cover, like stiff English butlers in old movies, think that almost any expression of feelings reeks of sentimentality. They wrinkle up their noses. People who weep easily, who attend funerals for recreation, may think that any expression of feelings, however exaggerated, is pretty much OK.

Yet the word *sentimentality*, so difficult to define, is the death ray in the literary critic's arsenal of weapons. Once a critic deploys it, entire books of poetry can be summarily vaporized. Since sentimentality cannot be objectively defined, no author can completely defend against it. The only way to be completely safe from the charge is to write with so much restraint that emotion is virtually excluded. And that of course leads to poetry that has no feeling, which has no "human heat," as my friend Jim Harrison says. The absence of emotion is not what we readers go to books of poetry for. We want some of that human heat. Each of us who writes must find a balance between restraint and expressions of feeling.

I once wrote to the late Richard Hugo, who from time to time had been accused of sentimentality. I told him of once having seen a silent film in which Charlie Chaplin played a night janitor in a department store. There was a mezzanine above the main floor, with no safety rail. The dark store lay far below. To impress the young woman who was with him, Chaplin roller-skated right on the edge of this chasm, flying along on one foot or the other, back and forth, smiling and waving, altogether oblivious of the danger of plunging over the edge. The entire movie audience held its breath with every pass.

I told Hugo I thought his best poems managed to skate along the edge of sentimentality without careening off the edge. Here is one of those poems:

➡ LETTER TO KATHY FROM WISDOM

My dearest Kathy: When I heard your tears and those of your
mother over the phone from Moore, from the farm
I've never seen and see again and again under the most
uncaring of skies, I thought of this town I'm writing from,
where we came lovers years ago to fish. How odd
we seemed to them here, a lovely girl and a fat
middle 40's man they mistook for father and daughter
before the sucker lights in their eyes flashed on. That was
when we kissed their petty scorn to dust. Now, I eat alone
in the cafe we ate in then, thinking of your demons, the sad
days you've seen, the hospitals, doctors, the agonizing
breakdowns that left you ashamed. All my other letter
poems I've sent to poets. But you, your soft round form
beside me in our bed at Jackson, you were a poet then,
curving lines I love against my groin. Oh, my tenderest

raccoon, odd animal from nowhere scratching for a home,
please believe I want to plant whatever poem will grow
inside you like a decent life. And when the wheat you've known
forever sours in the wrong wind and you smell it
dying in those acres where you played, please know
old towns we loved in matter, lovers matter, playmates, toys,
and we take from our lives those days when everything moved,
tree, cloud, water, sun, blue between two clouds, and moon,
days that danced, vibrating days, chance poem. I want one
who's wondrous and kind to you. I want him sensitive
to wheat and how wheat bends in cloud shade without wind.
Kathy, this is the worst time of day, nearing five, gloom
ubiquitous as harm, work shifts changing. And our lives
are on the line. Until we die our lives are on the mend.
I'll drive home when I finish this, over the pass that's closed
to all but a few, that to us was always open, good days
years ago when our bodies were in motion and the road rolled out
below us like our days. Call me again when the tears build
big inside you, because you were my lover and you matter,
because I send this letter with my hope, my warm love, Dick.

Some readers of this book will think Hugo went over the edge in
this poem, but I admire him for having taken the risk. I was never to
get a response to my letter because he died a few weeks later, but from
his essays on writing, I think he would have agreed. In his very useful
book on writing poetry, The Triggering Town, he suggests a poet must be
willing to risk sentimentality.

Because sentimentality is such a difficult word to define, let's use
gushiness. Most of us know when a poem is gushy. There is only one
kind of gushy, whereas there are as many kinds of sentimentality as
there are literary critics unsnapping their holsters and drawing out that
terrifying word.

Generally, though, it's best not to worry too much about sentimen-
tality, which nobody can clearly define and the notion of which, once
implanted in your head, can paralyze you like a wasp on the back
of a caterpillar. Instead, if you hold yourself back just short of what
you think is gushiness, that's enough restraint for first-draft poetry.

Then let your poem age for a few weeks and see if you don't see a little gushiness seeping out of the lines. That's the time, when you're revising your poem, for noticing that if you keep roller-skating along that course you're likely to wind up smashing down through the glass top of the cosmetics counter.

Here's another way of thinking about expressions of feeling. A poem is an object constructed of words, and when this object is presented to its readers, it is theirs to respond to however they wish. By carefully selecting the details, the poet can guide this response to some degree. For example, if into a scene a poet puts a blind child, the reader's response can be expected to be appropriate. Sentimentality can happen when a poet adds language, often as excessive modifiers, in an attempt to force a response, like, "That poor, miserable blind child with his wee white cane." Basically, a poet can avoid sentimentality by giving the reader credit for knowing how to respond to something without being led by the nose.

Let's take a look at this good example by Dixie Lee Partridge, our second poem about fish in aquariums:

⇒ FISH

It is suspended mid-tank,
fins wilted at edges like leaf curl
on a failing plant. Blood red dots the tail.

None of us knows whether it is sick
or old, the relative span of goldfish.
The children hold vigil, mid-night

wakes detoured from the bathroom
toward aquamarine light,
the magnified fish-eye

unmoved. Its gold
turns the color of flesh, then fades.
They discuss helping it die,

and how to, but no one wants to lift it
from faint liquid life
into the closing air.

They wait until the fourth day
when it stays, a pale float
curved at the surface.

Scooping it out with a silver bowl,
the three of them carry it
to the garden, each holding the rim.

Between corn and blackberries
they shape a hollow with their trowel,
pour in the fish and watch fluid

seep slowly downward
until the blanched form clings to soil,
a fetal arc still drawn to water.

After, they sketch
on the dry shoal with their stick
the shallows of a name.

One of the hardest things to learn is how poems can express strong
feelings without expressly stating those feelings. Part of the problem
is that in everyday conversation we often quite freely make statements
about feelings: "The kids' goldfish died and they *really* felt bad." In
this effective poem nowhere is there a statement of feeling unless we
want to fasten upon the rather weak "no one wants to lift it." The poem
begins with description and follows description all the way through,
letting the behavior of the participants show us how they feel. One
of this poem's really masterful touches, for me, is the image of the
children all holding onto the bowl, participating in the ritual of burial
as a little community. I know how to appropriately respond to that bit
of description, and have quite strong feelings about it without the poet
telling me how she wants me to feel.

Sometimes when working with beginning poets I tell them that they are
forbidden to write about their feelings. In other words, they cannot make
overt statements of feeling. This throws them back upon scene and
mood and pacing and other devices through which they must convey
their emotions. It's good discipline. You might try it.

Here's a short poem of mine in which I went out of the way to express the weight of a loss without stating it:

⏤◇ AFTER YEARS

> Today, from a distance, I saw you
> walking away, and without a sound
> the glittering face of a glacier
> slid into the sea. An ancient oak
> fell in the Cumberlands, holding only
> a handful of leaves, and an old woman
> scattering corn to her chickens looked up
> for an instant. At the other side
> of the galaxy, a star thirty-five times
> the size of our own sun exploded
> and vanished, leaving a small green spot
> on the astronomer's retina
> as he stood in the great open dome
> of my heart with no one to tell.

I wanted to show my readers how it feels to see, at a distance, a person one once loved, but I didn't want to come right out and say something like, "It really shook me up to see her." Instead, I developed a set of details to convey the emotion.

When it comes to expressing feelings, each of us knows not to walk right up to a total stranger on a street corner, somebody waiting for a light to change, and immediately say, "My lover just left me and I AM ABOUT READY TO FREAK OUT!" We know that if we did, the stranger would likely take off running against the red light. But if we're friendly, and casually draw that stranger into a conversation, then begin walking along with her, it may be possible to tell her how much trouble we're in by the time we get to the end of the next block.

It's not a bad idea to test the opening lines of your poems against this example, because that stranger, your reader, can quite easily be turned away by the first words you write. I wrote earlier about first impressions. It can be to your advantage to ease your reader along by not making too many demands, at least initially. Keep in mind that your reader, at the other end of the country, opening a literary journal to a page with your poem, is indeed a stranger, and like a stranger is slightly suspicious of what is before her. She's not your best friend, at least not yet, and you can't take it for granted that she's ready to welcome whatever you say.

Here's a beautiful poem by the late Jane Kenyon that addresses a private grief while standing at a distance from it. Many of us have had, or will have, the experience of wishing for a merciful death for an aging parent:

➡ IN THE NURSING HOME

She is like a horse grazing
a hill pasture that someone makes
smaller by coming every night
to pull the fences in and in.

She has stopped running wide loops,
stopped even the tight circles.
She drops her head to feed; grass
is dust, and the creekbed's dry.

Master, come with your light
halter. Come and bring her in.

Because making a comparison is a means of taking a step back from reality and then looking at it in a new way, the comparison in itself is a device of detachment and restraint. Without the comparison, in this instance an extended simile, this poem might have been nothing but raw emotion, even sentimentality.

(Note also the interesting use of double entendre, made possible by a deft use of a line ending: The next to the last line is first read as "Master, come with your light" as in "God, come with the light of eternal life." And then, after that touch of spirituality, we read on to the last line where "halter" draws us back down into a more practical or realistic state.)

Some poets have gotten the idea that they can say things about their feelings in poems that most of us wouldn't feel right about saying at the dinner table, as if writing a poem gives you permission to talk about things you wouldn't talk about in public. But we need to keep in mind that writing a poem is public, too. Your reader is right there on the other side of the table, politely and patiently listening to you. How long do you dare go on about the misery your hemorrhoids are causing you? Of course, if your imaginary reader is someone who *likes* poems about somebody else's hemorrhoids, well . . . My objection is to a kind of poem that feels to me as if it had been *motivated* by self-indulgence, a poem that puts the need of the poet to talk about himself or herself far out in front of the needs of the reader.

Perhaps there have always been people who took up writing poems just so they could talk about themselves, but self-indulgent poetry almost always disappears in time, a victim of its own failure to engage the needs and interests of others. It takes a grateful audience to keep a poem alive. Expression of feeling in poetry ought to be measured against the reader's tolerance for such expression.

CHAPTER SEVEN

Can You Read Your Poem through Your Poem?

When my sister and I were small children, perhaps five and eight years old, our parents took us to the Wisconsin Dells, a popular tourist attraction just a few hours' drive from my grandparents' home in northeastern Iowa. These picturesque rock palisades on the Wisconsin River are a smaller, flooded version of Colorado Springs' spectacular Garden of the Gods.

I remember very little of that trip, but we can be almost certain it was one of our family's daylong outings with a predictable lunch of cold-meat, mayonnaise, and Wonder Bread sandwiches. I have forgotten most of that day, and have long since lost whatever souvenirs I wheedled my dear parents into buying, trinkets that would have been paid for slowly and painfully, coin by coin, from a purse that my mother always held tightly in both hands. I probably went home with one of those little souvenir Indian tomahawks in my lap, one with a black rubber blade painted aluminum and a few brightly dyed chicken feathers tied around the handle. Or perhaps it was an Indian drum made of pieces of inner tube stretched by shoelaces over a cardboard cylinder.

But I do vividly remember going for a ride in an excursion boat that had a clear glass bottom. It floated with grace and ease and a throbbing gurgle across water brightly dappled with summer sunlight. Beneath the glass floor I could see fish swimming, catfish and carp and gar, and rocks eroded into imaginative shapes, and soda bottles that people on earlier cruises had dropped over the side.

I remember being completely absorbed by this underwater world until a large woman sitting nearby leaned over too far and her white-rimmed cat's-eye sunglasses slid off the end of her nose and fell with a clatter onto the glass. That sudden interference on the surface of the dreamy world beneath me brought my attention back to the glass floor, back to the ordinary world of being a little boy, hot and impatient and cross. The moment had been spoiled.

Enjoying a well-written poem can be like going for a ride in a glass-bottomed boat. The poet deftly and confidently pilots the language, taking the reader across sometimes deep, sometimes cold, often color-ful waters. The reader peers down through the clear floor of the poem, down through the page upon which words have been printed with type and ink, a page now magically gone transparent, into a fascinating realm revealed by the poem. The reader's experience in this world beneath the page is much like a dream, trancelike and timeless. His or her attention swims playfully among the waving grasses and mossy rocks of the poem, until something—a pair of sunglasses maybe—suddenly clatters down upon the surface and spoils the moment. You don't want that to happen.

You'll find all sorts of dropped sunglasses on the surface of poems. For example, here are just a couple I often come upon:

The ampersand—&—was invented by typesetters to enable them to make their lines of lead type a little shorter in length, so as to fit the horizontal restraints of narrow columns, and poets do sometimes use them for that reason, to shorten a line enough that it needn't be broken and dropped to the next line. But I never come upon an ampersand in a poem that doesn't hang me up for just an instant while I wonder why the poet decided to use it. There is really nothing wrong with the word "and," and it doesn't attract any attention, but every ampersand requires a reader to think about it, if only for a second. I'm sure plenty of readers are so accustomed to ampersands that they don't even notice them, and I'm probably a crank on this, but the use of any graphic symbol in place of a word is just a little risky.

Another stylistic trend in contemporary poetry is to drop articles, perhaps in an attempt to heighten the energy of the language. A poet might do something like this:

> CB radio blares, man shouts,
> dog growls . . .

There are times when writing like this can be effective, and times when a reader is brought up short, wondering why on earth a poet would choose to "talk" that way, to sound like a robot. The standard use of articles avoids this stylistic affectation and calls no attention away from the poem and to the poet's choices.

> A CB radio blares, a man shouts,
> a dog growls . . .

And so on. In your poetry reading you'll find all sorts of little things dropped on the glass.

But let's be a little more systematic. Here are some steps you can go through after you've finished drafting your poem, steps that can catch some of the things that might spoil the transparency of your writing.

Squint your eyes until you can't read the words but can still make out the shape of your poem on the page:

```
        XXXXXXXXXXXXXXXXXXXXX
        XXXXXXXXXXXXXXXXXX
        XXXXXXXXXXXXXXXXXXXXXX
        XXXXXXXXXXXXXXXXXX
        XXX
        XXXXXXXXXXXXXXXXXXXXXX
        XXXXXXXXXXXXXXXXXXXX
                XXXXXXXXXX
        XXXXXXXXXXXXXXXXX
        XXXXXXXXXXXXXXXXXXXX
```

Is there anything about that shape that is likely to make a reader stop, if only for a split second, to wonder what you were intending? Might it be line 5, that one short line, or line 8 with its deep indentation? My point is that if while being absorbed by the poem, the reader has to stop and think, "Why did the poet make that one line so short? Why's that line indented when none of the others are?" that reader has been drawn back to the surface of the page, to the floor of the excursion boat. In this instance, the risk is probably very slight because readers of poetry are used to lines of varying length and unconventional indentation, but the overall appearance of your poem is just one more thing you ought to think about during the process of revision.

While we're talking about shapes, let me say something about stanzas. Many contemporary poets choose to use, say, three-line stanzas, possibly because it makes the poem look more orderly and suggests a relationship to music. After all, we do talk about poems as "lyric." Whatever their reason, unless the stanzas make some sense as blocks of speech, like paragraphs in prose, they can call attention to themselves. Here, for example, is the way in which many poems are written today:

> Myrtle went downtown to the store
> to buy a bag of green beans for supper.
> While she was there she ran into
>
> her friend Marge, who had lost her
> checkbook. Marge said, "Oh, Myrtle,
> I'm so glad you came along because
>
> I didn't know what I was going to
> do. . . .

And so on. These stanzas call attention to themselves because they don't have any integrity as organized units of speech. The reader stops to think, why on earth is this poem chopped up like this? *Is it just to make it look like a poem?*

In business, executives make cost-benefit analyses. I used this term earlier. They never want the cost to exceed the benefit. Every choice you make in a poem, thinking to make it better, can also have a corresponding cost. If you want to make a line look shorter by using an ampersand or an abbreviation of a word, you face the cost of drawing the reader's attention back to the surface while he or she wonders why you decided to use *Sgn* for *surgeon*.

Don't be afraid to use the following devices, but give them a cost-benefit analysis:

- The use of unconventional grammar, spelling, capitalization or punctuation. One common instance is to use i for I, which is merely cute.

- The use of typographic devices like & or + to stand for "and" or "plus."
- Any unusual shape in the way the poem is laid out on the page.

You've undoubtedly seen many poems, even by famous poets, that include things like these, little things dropped on the glass. Almost all of the poems of e. e. cummings have them. Out of respect for cummings we still spell his name in lower case, as if he were watching. He dropped more sunglasses onto the surface of his poems than just about any other American poet, but there are many other poets who have played to a lesser or greater degree with the graphic elements of typography, experimental punctuation, grammar, etc., some to very good effect. But what you need to remember when composing your own poem is that while there may be a little *benefit* to using the lowercase i for the personal pronoun, there can also be a *cost*. The cost is the risk, however slight, that your reader will be drawn back to the surface to puzzle over your usage when you want his or her attention to be beyond the surface, peering down into the beautiful underwater garden of the poem.

Each of us must make a thousand choices in every poem. Nobody is going to take away your poetic license for playing with typography or punctuation or spelling. It can be lots of fun to write a poem about a flying seagull in the shape of a flying seagull, but you need to understand that that bird shape will interfere to some degree with the ability of the reader to pass through the surface into the poem behind that clever silhouette.

A shaped poem with a serious message will *never* be taken as seriously as the same poem without the trick of shape. A lovely elegy to your dead mother is not likely to be quite as moving as it might have been if you'd not shaped the typography to look like a coffin.

It may seem cool to leave out commas, to come up with a new spelling for a word, or to use an esoteric word, but if any of this forces your readers to back up and read a line again to see if they've understood, it costs you something. It may seem cool to allude to other literary works, to put in the name of a character from a Finnish saga, like Ilmarinen from *The Kalevala*, but if your reader has to put down the poem and go online to search Google for Ilmarinen, poof! there goes the transparency. You can, of course, explain in your poem who Ilmarinen is (if you can do it without weighing your poem down with exposition), and in that instance you can preserve some of the transparency.

We all know that there are experienced poetry readers who will know who Ilmarinen is, and who have read enough poetry that they are not going to be knocked off their ankles by unconventional grammar and punctuation. The question you have to answer, though, is, Where are those readers and how many of them are out there? The less risky your usage is, the better chance you have to get in touch with a broader audience. But if you want to write for your fellow poets at the Black Beret Coffeehouse, they will likely be much more accommodating of literary allusion and unconventional language. Or they'll pretend to be.

This notion of transparency in writing is not my own idea by any means. John Gardner wrote of it in his essays on writing fiction. And Robert Francis put it this way in his poem "Glass":

> Words should be looked through, should be windows.
> The best word were invisible.
> The poem is the thing the poet thinks.

Elsewhere in "Glass," Francis refers to "embossed glass," which he says "hides the poem or its absence." This is, of course, his allusion to the ornamentation of a poem with stylistic flourishes that call attention to themselves, or so I read it.

As I've suggested, there are many ways in which a poet can "emboss" a poem, intentionally or unintentionally, and spoil its transparency. Sometimes these distractions might be auditory, situations in which the poem's music—the sounds the words make in our heads—calls too much attention to itself. For example, it is very difficult to see through the surface of a poem embossed with heavy alliteration, like this bit of silliness from Algernon Charles Swinburne:

Black is the book of the bounty of old and its binding is blacker than bluer

That's a very good example of what Francis speaks of when he mentions that embossing can hide the poem's absence. Is there really a poem beneath the surface of Swinburne's lines, or is his poem "Nephilidia," from which this example comes, just an exercise in making noise?

But it is possible, of course, to employ a lot of noise—literary people like to call it music—and to create an effective and moving poem. One example of a famous poem whose surface is richly embossed with sound is this, from Gerard Manley Hopkins:

> I caught this morning morning's minion, king-
>> dom of daylight's dauphin, dapple-dawn-drawn Falcon, in his riding
>> Of the rolling level underneath him steady air, and striding
> High there, how he rung upon the rein of a wimpling wing
> In his ecstasy! Then off, off forth on swing,
>> As a skate's heel sweeps smooth on a bow-bend: the hurl and gliding
>> Rebuffed the big wind. My heart is hiding
> Stirred for a bird,—the achieve of, the mastery of the thing!

and so on. . . .

A great part of the charm of this excerpt from Hopkins's poem, written in 1877 and called "The Windhover," is its exhilaration and vitality. It is, I think, about exhilaration, about ecstasy. While Swinburne seemed to be trying to put one over on us with his noisy "Black is the book . . ." most of us who are adept at reading poems would agree that the exuberance of Hopkins's "The Windhover" comes right through the surface of the page. Despite the surface noise, the poem is transparent enough to let us see the exhilaration beneath. While reading we become part of the poem's excitement. Generations of readers have been entranced by dear, wacky Father Hopkins, whirling about in his words like a dervish in colorful, flying veils, showing us this amazing bird, but few people are moved by the poem by Swinburne because it seems as if he merely were writing to show us how very clever he could be. Another note to tack up over your desk: Too much cleverness in poetry can be a real killer.

But, as those who have attempted to teach the Hopkins poem have learned, a novice reader may fail to see through his richly modeled embossing into the poem beyond. The tightly wound music can present too much of an obstacle for such a reader. In the classroom, a deadly silence falls over the discussion. Eyes drop. You can almost hear the fingernails of the students trying to dig their way out of the poem.

I suggested earlier that every poem is in some sense an obstacle complete in itself, as are all works of art. It stands before us and must be negotiated with. Our willingness to work at that negotiation is based upon the degree to which the work of art has engaged our attention. Hopkins has done what all poets must do to some degree; he's selected a kind of audience by the manner in which he's written. His is a poem for more accomplished readers, not novices. When Hopkins did his cost-benefit analysis, he probably decided that the benefits to be achieved by his rich choice of rhythm and language were worth the cost of discouraging less sophisticated readers.

CHAPTER EIGHT

Writing from Memory

While we're at our desks writing and revising, we work from memory and the imagination, even though we may be writing about a parade of red ants we watched just a few moments before, a few feet from our back door. Memory is memory, and imagination is in part the reassembly of things we remember. Elsewhere I talk about writing from close observation. But here I want to talk about writing from distant memory, from events long past.

If you had a piggy bank the size of your head and filled it with nickels, you can imagine what it would weigh. A head is about that heavy. It is by volume the heaviest, most dense part of your body. On a platter, the head of John the Baptist would have weighed about as much as a good-sized Thanksgiving turkey.

Let's say a head weighs so much because it may contain, among thousands of other images, the Grand Canyon or the rolling sea off Cape Hatteras. Tons of colorful stone, or slate-gray crashing water. Think how much just those two vistas weigh, complete with the heavy tourist traffic, thousands of screaming gulls, and the frightened look your little daughter had on her face when they brought her first lobster and set it before her, claws and all. The big bang theory of the origin of the universe posits that everything came from a single, extremely dense speck. Everything was packed in there. This is just the way the brain is, and everything you know is stuffed inside.

Walt Whitman said he contained multitudes, and he certainly put a lot of what he contained into *Leaves of Grass*. But he must have left out a lot. There are just so many things you can fit into a poem, even into a great book of poems like *Leaves of Grass*.

Let's say you fleshed out your memories of all the people you know, your family, your friends, and all the people you've known who have disappeared into the past, just using the ones whose names you can remember. If your Uncle Jack was six-foot-ten, stand him in your front yard at full height, and put the old woman with the walker right next to him, and her little Boston terrier, and the niece with the red curly hair. At full height and weight, remember. If you did this with the memory of each person whose name you can remember, you'd soon see that your front yard isn't going to contain them. They'd be spilling over into the street, then covering the street and blocking the ice cream truck that you just remembered, then standing on your neighbors' freshly watered lawn. You'd have to lead them to a bigger place. What a parade, and more people coming by the minute! Maybe the high school football stadium would be big enough. I think I could put all the people I remember into a space like that, if at some point I decided to quit remembering people that popped into my mind: Oh, yes, and then there was that boy—what was his name? oh, yes, Lester Warren—whose bicycle got stolen. . . .

Then think about all the buildings you remember walking past, houses, stores, banks, filling stations. Reconstruct those buildings at full size and place them side by side and up and down a series of streets. Maybe there's a courthouse in a square, with buildings all around it, and then street after street, spreading out under the trees.

And then all those vistas you've taken in. Here's a cornfield, flashing green, crackling with midsummer; and here's the Sonoran Desert; and the Sawtooth Mountains. You've got to make space for all those vistas, and it's going to take a whole country to fit them in. The more you think of, the more memories there are.

Even I, who have never been to Europe or even seen every state in the Union, even I need a pretty big space for all the vistas, the people, the buildings. Maybe my country is only as big as the states of Nebraska and Iowa, but yours could be bigger. And all of that right in your head! No wonder it's so very heavy and it feels so good to rest it on a pillow.

If you are open to a short safari into the Country of Memory, just fifteen minutes will give you enough things to write about to last all morning, or all afternoon if you are an afternoon writer. And you don't have to leave your cup of coffee and your comfortable chair. Flannery

O'Connor said that enough has happened to each of us by the time we're eight years old for us to write about it forever.

One morning while I was writing, for example, I set out for a short jaunt through memory and wound up in front of a house on a shady street in Lincoln, Nebraska, a very small corner of my country of memory. My first wife and I once lived there, in a first-floor, one-bedroom apartment. She taught school while I was a graduate student. On this day in memory, I was shirking my scholarly responsibilities and writing a poem when I should have been starting a paper on *Paradise Lost*. I was never much good at doing what I was supposed to when it came to being educated.

In that country of memory I sat for a while, chewing my pencil, my notebook crawling with ideas. Such pleasure. The plastic curtains that came with the apartment lifted a little, wafted away by a cold draft from a crack at the base of the sash, and I could smell my wife's herbal shampoo from the nearby bathroom. The radio was playing something classical, but I couldn't have told you the composer's name then and I can't today. Then Herb Burton, who owned the local FM station, interrupted in his sonorous voice to say that the president had been shot in Dallas. And in the Country of Memory, November 1963, I looked around for somebody to tell but no one was there.

Writing about places that meant something to us can reach deeply within us. Here is Yehuda Amichai:

➻ I WALKED PAST A HOUSE WHERE I LIVED ONCE

I walked past a house where I lived once:
a man and a woman are still together in the whispers there.
Many years have passed with the quiet hum
of the staircase bulb going on
and off and on again.

The keyholes are like little wounds
where all the blood seeped out. And inside,
people pale as death.

I want to stand once again as I did
holding my first love all night long in the doorway.
When we left at dawn, the house

began to fall apart and since then the city and since then
the whole world.

I want to be filled with longing again
till dark burn marks show on my skin.

I want to be written again
in the Book of Life, to be written every single day
till the writing hand hurts.

When people get old and forgetful, we speak of their loss of short-
term or long-term memory. Short-term memory is made up of things
that might matter quite a bit at the moment—some errand that needs
to be run, some bill to be paid—but over the long course of a life these
minor activities aren't at all memorable and it's no wonder they're easy
to forget. Sure, it can be frustrating to send your elderly father to the
store for a loaf of bread and have him come home with a sack of overripe
plums. Maybe that instance goes into the vast reaches of your country of
memory even though it doesn't go into his. But how fortunate it is for
all of us that the long-term memory is the most durable. We each have
our country of memory always within us, always open to exploration,
and we hold this for most of our lives.

You happen to think of some object or event from the past, maybe
the clock in your grandmother's kitchen, and suddenly part of your
memory opens like a little door and you can see all kinds of other
details. The surface of memory is like one of those Advent calendars
with lots of little flaps under which you can see things.

Writing a poem about that clock, you begin to see all manner of
things: blue willow-ware dishes in the cupboards; a gray spatterware
colander on the countertop; the faucet dripping into a rusty stain in the
porcelain sink; your grandmother's soapy red hands; the fragrance of
cinnamon rolls fresh from the oven; the bull terrier, Ralph, gnawing on
a pork chop bone in the doorway; an autumn day outside the window
and the warm highway wavering beyond, upon which an old red truck
with one green door is passing, heaped with shelled corn, scarves of
cornhusks flying behind. And beyond that, the picked fields reaching
to the horizon. Wow! And all from just stepping into a memory to take
a close look at a clock.

You take pleasure in remembering first one thing and then another and another, your memory synapses all firing, pop, pop, pop. Some of the things you'll remember just won't fit into your poem. "Oh," you say, "I hadn't thought about that ugly umbrella stand for ten years and now I see I can't quite make it work in this poem! And I was so proud of myself for remembering it!"

But in this example you are still writing a poem about the kitchen clock, a cheap, round electric clock with a chrome ring and a noisy motor that growls all day like Ralph the bull terrier. Just because you suddenly remember that umbrella stand or perhaps that your grandfather always kept a deck of pinochle cards in the drawer to the left of the sink, doesn't mean the umbrella stand or the cards belong in the poem about the clock. If you want to hang onto your memory of the pinochle cards, a little sticky from players who had been eating orange rolls, go ahead and put the cards in the first draft and come back to them later. But don't think that just because you thought of these things while thinking about the clock means that the cards and umbrella stand ought to be in the final draft of the poem, unless of course they can be fully integrated or perhaps have taken over as the true subjects of the poem. It's just possible—and it often happens—that the poem turns out to be about the umbrella stand after all, or about the pinochle cards, and in the final draft the clock gets thrown out, never again to be heard growling from high on the wall. You have to trust in the process of writing to lead you toward the heart of the poem, and maybe the heart is one of the hearts in the pinochle deck. Sometimes you'll find out during revision that there was more than one poem in that room in your memory. The poem of the pinochle deck, another about the clock, and so on.

No matter which way your poem seems to be going, it can't hurt to get all the detail into the first draft, everything that comes to mind, every piece of silverware in the drawer, every crumb in the bottom of the cookie jar. Then you can go back and stroll through that room, like walking between overloaded tables at an estate sale. Carry the little basket of your poem and pick up only those details that you really want to use. The rest of the room is in your notebook, and still somewhere in your memory, and you can enjoy sitting there eating that hot cinnamon roll at another time. Unless Ralph snatches it out of your mind.

Here's a lovely little memory poem by Frank Steele, who, with his wife, Peggy, also a poet, lives in retirement in Bowling Green, Kentucky. I chose it in part because he uses "I remember" in it, and that seemed appropriate for what I've been talking about.

►◆ PARENTS

I felt his death coming for years
the way you can be under
fluorescent lights in a library
with no windows, reading
some bright page, and gradually
feel the sky outside
invisibly cloud over. But I remember
those last few times before his fall
how they would be standing in the driveway
waving goodbye again, how they lit up
for a moment, suddenly not old but just
themselves, his arm around her, cheering us on,
cheering for life itself as we drove away.

How much of his memories of this moment do you suppose Frank Steele intentionally left out? Surely all of his recollections would have taken up pages and pages, but he has selected just enough. Let's look at the details he has selected to work with.

This is at first look a simple, straightforward poem, clear and accessible, but I want to call your attention to the careful artistry in the subtle way Steele uses light. In the midst of life—that bright page that by its nature takes us away from the passage of time—comes an intimation of mortality, a faintly felt clouding over, a shadowing.

To use light as a symbol for life and darkness as a symbol for death aren't original usages, you might well argue, but their management in this poem is indeed original, with the invisible clouds casting shadows over a library, affecting the speaker inside, reading.

Steele suggests that the span of our lives is not all brightness and youth and then, all of a sudden, utter darkness, old age, and death. Instead it is more like a sky with drifting, broken clouds, sometimes letting a shaft of light down, a little touch of youth and vitality even in advanced age, just as it does toward the end of the poem, where the parents are lit for a moment, waving their family on into the future.

And notice how much is accomplished with that single word, *again*, in the tenth line: waving goodbye *again*, as if the parents might be depended upon to be there always, always ready to cheerfully wave the children on, though we understand that there will come a time when that brightly lit farewell will no longer be waiting. This is a good example of paring a poem to its essentials: the word *again* is enough. Steele didn't have to write

> But I remember
> those last few times before his fall
> how they would be standing in the driveway
> waving goodbye again, *just like they always*
> *stood there waving,* how they lit up
> for a moment, suddenly not old but just
> themselves, his arm around her, cheering us on,
> cheering for life itself as we drove away.

which would have made the poem feel a little looser, less controlled.

Steele doesn't feel the need to give us the particulars of the father's death. He uses that one word, *fall*, to carry the weight, and it is an especially good choice, too, because *fall* has an appropriate literal meaning—it could have been a real fall, for old people do fall—and a deeper meaning as well: fall as in a sudden decline. But, after all, the manner in which a person dies, the little details of an autopsy, say, whether the corpse has spots on its liver or lungs, doesn't in any way cancel the loss. Steele knows that his readers will not be more moved by knowing exactly how his father died. It is the loss of the father, that final unalterable absence, that touches us. He doesn't need to say

> But I remember
> those last few times before his fall
> *from a sudden cerebral vascular accident*
> how they would be standing in the driveway

The brevity of this poem is interesting in one other way: A grieving person, speaking of the loss of his parents, is quite likely, in an attempt to control his emotions, to keep his words to a minimum, to *bite off his words*, as we say. Sure, there are people who go on at great length lamenting the deaths of loved ones, but sometimes we get the impression that all that talk is mostly to draw attention to the suffering of the survivor rather than to honor the memory of the departed. Steele's poem attracts only a modest amount of attention to Steele, and devotes itself almost wholly to honoring the memory of the parents, "just themselves," as he says.

There are thousands of poems drawn from the past like this one, and then there are stories drawn from the past, just stories that haven't attained the stature of poetry because their authors haven't put quite enough pressure on them, haven't been careful enough in their selection of detail, haven't used rhythm and syntax and metaphor to heighten their effect. They haven't written them with the kind of *care* that Frank Steele has given his.

Good writing of all kinds requires this kind of care, this careful, meticulous selection. Let me show you a snippet of prose from a novel by Bonnie Burnard, *The Good House* (Henry Holt, 1999), that is as well written as any poem: You couldn't change a word of it without lessening its effect.

First, though, let me place the passage in context: A young mother, Sylvia, slowly dying of cancer, has been confined to a bed on the first floor of their house, and the family's friends and neighbors have volunteered to build a small bathroom off the kitchen so that she won't have to climb the stairs to the bathroom on the second floor. Sylvia's mother has come to help out, and she has at the time of this passage not been described. Notice how her actions here tell us so much about her and the way she feels about her daughter's illness. Here is a complete human being created within a few carefully written sentences:

> Sylvia's mother stripped the old kitchen wallpaper and burned it in the barrel down by the creek. She stayed with the paper as it burned, using the crowbar to push it down and down again into the fire. Waiting for the fire to do its work, she pulled her thick old cardigan tight and turned to watch the rush of the cold April creek on its way to the lake.

That repetition, to push the paper down and down again into the fire, is pure poetry.

THE USE OF ANECDOTE

Now I want to say a few more things about the necessity to do something more with memories than to just write them down and think that they're poems.

Not all poems tell stories, but many are narrative, that is, they follow a sequence of events over a period of time. We poets are social creatures, and we like to tell others about our experiences. The personal anecdote is so common in conversation as to be almost inextricable from it. Listen in on any group of people and you're very likely to hear someone say something like, "The other day, I was walking past Ed Schmidt's house, when all of a sudden . . ." In some conversations, a single anecdote becomes the subject, with the participants subsequently discussing the significance of that one story, and in others, the entire conversation may be little more than a round of anecdotes told in turn with a touch of competitiveness: "That's interesting, all right, but you'll never believe what happened to me the other day!"

All of us are accustomed to telling and listening to anecdotes, and anecdotal poems seem not all that far removed from the experience of daily conversation. In recent years, more and more poems have taken on an anecdotal manner. Because young poets look to available models for direction, it is no wonder that we see more little stories in verse published every year. I'd estimate that out of every hundred poems appearing in literary magazines today, ninety of them could be classed as personal anecdotes.

Because the common anecdote is most often spoken or told rather than being written down, the anecdote has never been accorded the honor of being deemed a recognized literary genre. The major genres, as you know, are drama, poetry, fiction, and nonfiction. Recently, creative nonfiction—nonfiction that employs fictive techniques—has been put forth as a candidate for canonization among the major genres, but no one yet has put forward the humble anecdote, which does indeed have a recognizable form and could be given its own category. Instead, anecdotes have been thought of as merely slight, as minor parts of fiction and nonfiction, as tools or devices to be employed in moving a larger story or theme forward or, due to their familiarity, for brightening an essay, biography, or memoir. They've been classed with the sketch and the vignette, considered a part and not a whole.

The only genre that the anecdote has to some degree insinuated itself into and then seized substantial control over is poetry. I'm not certain when this began to happen, but I've noticed an increasing proliferation of anecdotal poems for at least twenty-five or thirty years. There have always been short narrative poems, of course, but never as many as we see today. Perhaps poetry in recent years has grown too weak to resist the attractive, familiar, conversational, seductive anecdote, too eyesore from trying to describe actions, too weary of meditation and contemplation, too jaded by trying to present deeper poems to a largely indifferent audience.

I think it more likely that poets picked up on the anecdotal model and discovered that such poems were relatively easy to write and publish, since publishers dream of customers and the journal- and book-buying audience can be expected to go for little stories. Sometimes after reading a literary journal chock full of poems that are little more than anecdotes made to look like poems, I'm reminded of those sci-fi films in which a seed gets in under the skin of some innocent person, incubates into a monster, then bursts roaring from the belly of its host.

Readers of the late twenty-first century, looking back at a broad sample of our poetry after a hundred years' winnowing, may likely conclude that most of our poets were attempting to elevate the everyday personal anecdote to acceptability as a work of art. Take any dozen current literary journals or new collections of verse, and you'll quickly observe how many poems are merely plainspoken anecdotes tricked out in lines of verse. It is not at all unusual to find a volume of poems that consists of nothing but fifty or sixty two-minute narratives, often about a family or a marriage or . . . well, you know what I mean.

This popular means of writing lends much contemporary poetry a folksy, cracker-barrel tone, which fits nicely with the character of to-day's public poetry readings, which are not far removed from stand-up comedy routines, the speaker at center stage, telling brief, entertaining, sometimes embarrassing stories. The comic Bob Newhart, with his deadpan delivery, could make it big on the university poetry circuit today. Poets, preparing for readings, choose the works that are likely to entertain their audience, not their best poems but the ones that "work best."

And when it comes to the printed page, the traditional venue, we can see our poets—who may be the core of what's left of the audience for poetry—amusing each other within the warm and comfortable crossroads store of the literary quarterly, their chairs drawn close to the cast-iron English Department stove as they swap a few stories.

Opening our books of poems a hundred years from now, will readers see us poets in this way, as authors of anecdotes, and if so, so what? After all, we compose these poetic anecdotes for good reasons: We value our personal experiences (the Romantics taught us to do that), readers and listeners can be relied upon to respond warmly to a story well told, we have successful models to emulate, and—very important—most editors have become accustomed to and are comfortable with publishing anecdotes-as-verse.

But something seems to be missing.

It isn't the lack of form, because there is a form to the everyday anecdotal poem. Its form is a narrative sequence: "Whenever Grandma peeled potatoes / she got out her paring knife, and then . . ." And in nearly all the anecdotal poetry published today, you can count on, after a sequence of narrative particulars, a last-minute *one, two, three, heave-ho!* as the poet attempts to generate some kind of special weight in the concluding lines:

> This happened first,
> and then this
> happened; then this
> and this; this happened
> next, then this
> and this and this,
> and then—you won't
> believe it—
> THIS!

A variant on the final line is "Thisssssssssssssssssssss . . ." in those poems that attempt to gain in dramatic effect by fading away into silence. I recently read a jacket blurb that said "there is a remarkable

intensity of voice that keeps the poem moving beyond the last line."
Uh-huh.

This final heave-ho—is it necessitated by the poet's need to concentrate energy behind a final closure, or is it a relic from a time when the poem proceeded toward a closing message of instruction? Do we now conclude poems with the heave-ho because we feel guilty about not having come to any real conclusion? Or might the anecdote poem conclude as it does simply because *oral* anecdotes conclude this way—with the storyteller pouncing upon the punch line at the end. Hurrah! Whatever the reason, this last heave-ho is an integral part of the anecdotal form, and sometimes it works and sometimes it doesn't.

It isn't the lack of a sense of prosody, or a shortage of beautiful and moving effects. Many of these anecdote poems have such effects. In the hands of a talented poet, an anecdote can rise above itself, can touch us deeply and alter our perception of the world. The Chinese poets call this "lifting the eyes," meaning that at some point the poet looks up from the triggering subject and sees (or senses) something larger.

⇥ THE ENVOY

> One day in that room, a small rat.
> Two days later, a snake.
>
> Who, seeing me enter,
> whipped the long stripe of his
> body under the bed,
> then curled like a docile house-pet.
>
> I don't know how either came or left.
> Later, the flashlight found nothing.
>
> For a year I watched
> as something—terror? happiness? grief?—
> entered and then left my body.
>
> Not knowing how it came in,
> Not knowing how it went out.
>
> It hung where words could not reach it.
> It slept where light could not go.

Its scent was neither snake nor rat,
neither sensualist or ascetic.

There are openings in our lives
of which we know nothing.

Through them
the belled herds travel at will,
long-legged and thirsty, covered with foreign dust.

Poems like this one by Jane Hirshfield use the anecdote as a substructure for deep and meaningful writing, and in such instances the poet is not the slave but the master of the short narrative, using it in the same ways that a novelist might, as part of something greater. I find so tiring those thousands of poems in which the anecdote is wholly in charge, has seized control of the total effect, poems in which some personal story has fleshed itself out in the guise of a poem and demonstrates no aspiration to be anything greater. *A poem must be something more than an anecdote arranged in lines.* Yet artful composition, like that in Hirshfield's poem, can elevate an anecdote into true poetry.

Here's one by Henry Taylor:

➡◈ THE HAYFORK

I could get up from this kitchen table, I think,
and go see for myself whether, even now,
in the worn planks of the old barn floor,
there might be two holes I saw made there
forty years ago, in a single second along
the ponderous time-line of farming. Well,

I might get over there one of these days.
Meanwhile, what can I see from here? We entered
the barn's second story through a big sliding door
at the top of an earthen ramp. There was a haymow
on either side of a wagon-wide aisle-way.
A rail under the ridgepole ran gable to gable.

High in a dark far end, when I was a boy,
the old hayfork still hung there, barely visible

in cobwebs and thin strips of sunlight
that burst between weathering boards. Shaped
like a three-foot inverted U, a giant staple,
it rusted toward absolute darkness against which

stark blobs left by last season's mud-wasps
stood out like white spots on a heifer.
Who knew how long it had been there? Loose hay
was giving way to bales before I was born,
though here and there I've seen it made, the teams
of work-horses pulling the loader and wagon,

a man with a pitchfork working everyday magic
on top of the rack, the slow ride to the barn,
drawing the load up under the rail and the trip-stop.
A man dragged the fork down, hauling against
the tow-rope's weight the forty pounds of steel
with two barbed ends that grabbed the wads of hay.

Then the team, unhitched from the wagon, pulled
on the tow-rope, moving away from the barn,
lifting the hay toward the roof. A click
as the trolley-hook caught, then the hay
rode back along the rail into the mow
where men forked it away for the winter.

So to a day when I was twelve or thirteen,
when the baled hay we were making was plentiful,
stacked in the mow almost up to the roof,
and we were standing around in the aisle-way
after the wagon backed out, catching breath,
getting ready to go back to the field. One man

up in the mow took a notion and snatched
at the tag-end of rope still fastened to the hayfork,
so it whirred down the track to a place just above
the middle of the aisle-way, hit the trip, and dropped,
all faster, it seemed, than the noise of the track
could make us look up, and plunged its two points

into the floor just beside the left foot of Joe Trammel,
who stood there, leaning away from it, looking down
and then up, and around at all of us, a barnful
of men struck reverently silent in the presence
of whatever it was, the good luck that kept Joe
from injury, the bad luck that gave him his worst scare

in years, the innocent thoughtlessness that led
to that yank on the rope, the way things can go
for years without happening, biding their time
in a dust-whirling, cobwebby barn I can see
and smell and hear right now, staring down
at the grain in the wood of this kitchen table.

Let's imagine the core anecdote here, the one we'd expect to hear in
conversation. It might go something like this:

> When I was a boy, there was a heavy old overhead hayfork
> in our barn, maybe three feet long, the kind that moved on
> a track and was made to drop down and spear up loads of
> hay and haul them back into the loft. One day we were in
> there working and a guy who wasn't thinking jerked on the
> trip rope and that thing came down and just barely missed
> another guy. It stuck right in the floor at his feet, ker-chunk!

The kind of anecdotal poem I'm objecting to would simply take this
little story, using the same words and word order and make it look like
a poem:

⇢ THE HAYFORK

> When I was a boy there was
> a heavy old overhead hayfork
> in our barn, maybe three feet long,
> the kind that moved on a track
> and was made to drop down
> and spear up loads of hay
> and haul them back into the loft.
> One day we were in there working

and a guy who wasn't thinking
jerked on the trip rope
and that thing came down
and just barely missed
another guy. It stuck right
in the floor at his feet,
ker-chunk!

That *ker-chunk* at the end is meant to give us the feeling that there's a significant moment at the close, and if you look at a lot of contemporary poems you'll see a lot of *ker-chunks* like that, words or phrases tacked onto the end to make us feel that the poem has ended with force and resolution.

But look at what Henry Taylor does with the anecdote as a substructure. Here are some of the moments I find to be notable, not in any order of significance:

First, he establishes a distinctive and engaging speaker. Within a few lines Taylor creates a character in whose unique voice we will hear the story, and this speaker is as important to the effect of the poem as is the hayfork anecdote. This is not just any old voice delivering an anecdote. We are instead being introduced to a multidimensional man, a talented tale-spinner, his voice colloquial and canny in its way of drawing out his story and sustaining our interest. Every word in Taylor's poem will seem appropriate to the voice of this man, who speaks in the vernacular of rural life. He says "one man / . . . took a notion," and that things go on "biding their time." This characterization of a unique speaker is part of the artfulness of this poem.

Robert Frost has a character like this in one of his narrative poems, "The Witch of Coös," which you may have read. An old woman tells a stranger an intriguing story about a corpse in her cellar, and she says in her own distinctive, colloquial voice that for proof she's got one of the finger bones in her button box. But she doesn't show the finger bone any more than Taylor's character shows us the holes in the floor.

Next, Taylor uses suspense. Notice how by the end of the second stanza we're already interested in hearing what will happen, and by the end of the third stanza we get the inkling that what is going to happen has something to do with the hayfork. Its description, "a three-foot inverted U, a giant staple," hints at its danger. Later it's described as heavy, adding to that threat.

The poem is set up in stanzas, with metrical variance that stays pretty close to five beats per line, and this form has an effect on the reader, suggesting order and providing a quiet, rhythmic music. Deft use of form is much like the background score of a motion picture; it ties the film together, induces subtle effects, yet is not so pronounced as to get in the way of the narrative. On the matter of the effects of the order and logic suggested by form, P. D. James, the English mystery writer, suggested in a television interview that the reason people read mysteries in which every loose end gets tied up at the conclusion is because they find this to be a reassurance that despite what we perceive to be random violence and chaos, the world is indeed a place of order.

There are dozens of deft artistic choices in "The Hayfork." Notice, for example, the careful repetition and arrangement of vowel sounds, the occasional true, slant, and near rhymes like "shaped" with "staple." And I do want to point to one of my favorite moments: After almost eight full stanzas that set the dusty, lofty stage through which the hayfork will drop, we learn the specific name of the man who was nearly struck, Joe Trammel. That name, the only name other than the "I" of the speaker, one name out of all the men present, is as specific a location, as it were, as are the two holes left in the floor. Had there been other names mentioned throughout the poem, this one name wouldn't have had such a profound effect. Joe Trammel is memorialized forever, and the whole story, as it were, is a frame around his name. We know nothing of him but that he was the one standing closest, and yet he is suddenly and indelibly the one made vivid and immortal.

Where's the ker-chunk in Taylor's poem? Well, there isn't one. Ker-chunk is the cheap way out of a story, the easy way. Instead, Taylor brings us back to the kitchen table, and the character of the storyteller, whose persona and storytelling style are really the subjects of the poem.

Look again at the poem about the rattlesnake by Brewster Ghiselin on page 32. It is at base an anecdote. In the most common form of the anecdote, an adventurer goes to an unknown place and returns to tell the community about an interesting experience. This poem conforms to that tradition: The speaker comes upon a rattlesnake, kills it, and comes to the community of readers to tell about the experience.

Had Ghiselin's poem ended with the line

> In the dead beads of the tail

it would remain more anecdote than poem, its story told, the snake dead. But Ghiselin knows that poetry goes beyond mere anecdote, that it transcends the simple telling of an occurrence. In the last three lines we see him using a simile to move out and away from his very close focus on the dead snake, taking in a broader vista:

> In the dead beads of the tail
> Fade, as wind fades
> From the wild grain of the hill.

We feel a lifting as these last lines fall into place, feel swept up and away. The death of the snake is like a pebble dropped into a pond, from which ripples spread. One death, even that of a poisonous snake, thus spreads out to touch the world. Unless something like this happens in an anecdotal poem, the poem fails as poetry.

Here's one more example. In the following poem Thomas Lux works with the unique reading of events and manner of speaking of a voice altogether different from that of the poet:

●◇ SHAVING THE GRAVEYARD

> The graveyard being what he called his face;
> even as a young man
> he called his face the graveyard—he talked
> like that, funny, odd
> things that scared me sometimes
>
> in our early years. I thought maybe he was a little touched
> (his uncle Bob was certifiable)
> but it was just his way of talking. U-*feeisms*,
> he told me once, he liked to use u-*feeisms*,
> which was no language
>
> I ever heard of. He never touched a drop, though,
> nor ever lifted a hand against me
> or the kids, and when it came to loving,

well, he was sweet, but talking strange then
too: Bug Sauce, he'd call me, or Lavender Limbs,

or sometimes Birdbath—never Honey
or Sugar like other husbands when they talked, talked.
He was funny like that. Anyway,
after breakfast (he always shaved *after* breakfast,
said his face was "looser" then)

he'd stroke his chin and say:
Time to shave the graveyard,
and he would and then he'd go to work,
the handle of his lunchpail hooked through
with a belt and slung

over his shoulder. Some days I'd watch him
until he reached the corner
of Maple and Cottage
where he turned and walked the two blocks
to the mill.

Lux adds interest to this anecdote by capturing the woman's voice,
with its touches like *u-feeisms* as well as her own fascination with the way
in which her husband talked. Notice how she comments on his manner
of speaking again and again: "he talked / like that, funny, odd . . . but
it was just his way of talking . . . never Honey / or Sugar like other
husbands when they talked, talked. / He was funny like that." And of
course we can read the poem as a veiled comment about how poets
relate to their readers, in this example the husband/poet talking in his
peculiar manner, the wife/audience charmed by those peculiarities.

Just as happens in everyday conversations, it's the *manner* of relating
an anecdote that distinguishes yours from every other. If you choose to
write poems like this, don't rely on just the details of a good story to lift
it into poetry. You need to do more than that. Think about the speaker's
characteristic voice, the syntax, the rhythm, the form, the selection of
details. The story itself is merely the material. You have to do something
special with that material if you want it to be a poem.

CHAPTER NINE

Working with Detail

You're talking to somebody who says, "Those were the good old days," and you ask, "So, what was so good about them?" and they say, "Well, I don't know . . . I guess we had a lot of fun." And you say, "What kind of fun?" and they say, "Oh, you know, family picnics and holidays." And you say, "Give me an example of something fun that happened at a family picnic," and they say, "Well, OK . . . I remember one time when my Aunt Mae used termite powder in a layer cake, thinking it was sugar." At that point, the conversation begins to get interesting.

In conversation and in our writing we tend to generalize, to summarize, to say things like "Those were the good old days," but as writers, if we want to engage our listeners and readers, we need to shake off generalization and go for the specifics. It's the details that make experiences unique and compelling. It's watching one particular old woman in a cardigan sweater burn wallpaper in a barrel, pushing it down and down with a crowbar. After you've written each draft of your poem, take a look at it to see if your detailing is as good as it might be. Have you included the details that are unique to your experience?

PAYING ATTENTION

The poet Linda Gregg asks her students to take a close look at just six things each day. What seems like a simple discipline turns out to be quite difficult because, by habit, most of us go through our lives without paying much attention to anything. Surely it's happened to you: at the end of a day, you drive several miles home and when you get there you can't remember a thing you saw along the way. Making an effort to *pay attention* to what's going on around them works for Linda Gregg's students and it will work for you.

Memory and the imagination are excellent tools when it comes to creating a setting, for example, but it's *observed* details that really make a poem vivid.

Immediately following September 11, 2001, a poem by Stephen Dunn about a terrorist—written some time before the event—began to pinball its way around the World Wide Web, while thousands of poets, skilled and amateur alike, sat down to write poems of their own. Much of what got written, even by our most accomplished poets, wasn't very compelling, mostly because it was based upon the nation's common, collective, *general* experiences of that day—images of the towers burning and falling; the Pentagon with its gaping black wound; the red, white, and blue flapping over the smoking rubble—and not upon each poet's specific, personal experience of that morning: how the breakfast eggs went cold on the plate and the coffee went sour in the cup. The large is present in the small, and the better poem might have been the one in which the poet finds herself at a specific corner gas station in Kansas, holding her daughter's bicycle tire in one hand, under a suddenly empty sky.

An issue of *Poetry* magazine, published a few months after the events of September 11, was almost totally devoted to poems about terror. Of these I liked best "Searchers" by D. Nurkse, a poet who lives in Brooklyn. It's a poem that really pays attention.

I had read elsewhere, some weeks after the attack, that the rescue dogs at the World Trade Center got badly depressed because they couldn't find any living bodies in the rubble, so people hid in the ruins and let the dogs find them. Nurkse's poem begins:

> We gave our dogs a button to sniff,
> or a tissue, and they bounded off
> confident in their training,
> in the power of their senses
> to recreate the body,
>
> but after eighteen hours in rubble
> where even steel was pulverized

> they curled on themselves
> and stared up at us
> and in their soft huge eyes
> we saw mirrored the longing for death . . .

Notice how tightly this poem is focused: button, tissue, the eyes of the dogs. We are at the dusty, smoky foot of the damaged Manhattan skyline, in the midst of thousands of rescue workers and scores of TV personalities, and we are taking a close look at the dogs.

The poem continues:

> then we had to beg a stranger
> to be a victim and crouch
> behind a girder, and let the dogs
> discover him and tug him
> proudly, with suppressed yaps,
> back to Command and the rows
> of empty triage tables.

And it concludes:

> But who will hide from us?
> Who will keep digging for us
> here in the cloud of ashes?

My late friend, the novelist Warren Fine, on the day of a much-trumpeted full solar eclipse, drove out to a park to see how the animals would behave as the light slid away. While everybody else in Nebraska was staring at the sun through exposed photographic negatives, Warren was off by himself, watching the birds flap to their roosts and the buffalo lie down to sleep. He knew the value of specific, concrete observation, of paying attention to what was going on right under his nose. He knew to keep his attention on the specifics and to let the grand subjects emerge from carefully observed particulars. The most effective poetry is not likely to be built from a sweeping look at an enormous panorama. It will more likely be found in watching a dog sniff a button.

There are those who think poets are more sensitive than other people, more keenly aware of the world, but most of the poets I know are just as oblivious to what's happening around them as is the rest of the population. Henry James advised writers, "Be one of those on whom nothing is lost." That's what you need to teach yourself.

Here's a poem by David Ray:

➡ AT THE TRAIN STATION IN PAMPLONA

the girl sitting on the bench and the
man standing above her with his hands
hopelessly in his pockets are having
a hard time of it. His eyes are almost
as red as hers are and he goes on saying
things with a kind of run-down version
of his usual charm. But she's fed up,
and looking between overcoats, toying
with the green umbrella, in a smoke-
filled station is one more way of
keeping from crying. She gets up
to leave with a vengeance. His hand
touches hers, and he makes her smile
once more, using torture. She'd still
die for him. She reads his face again
like a book she's put down a thousand
thousand times. Now she obeys
and steps up onto that wooden train
past numbers painted gold. This
is a train heading through mountains.
When she settles herself by the window
she is already broadcasting to other
men the message of her helplessness.

For the past fifty years, or thereabouts, readers of contemporary poetry have grown more and more accustomed to poems about the poet, poems in which the personal pronoun "I" is preeminent. We sometimes call this "confessional poetry" because the poet bares his or her soul, confessing to this or that. The poet is at center stage; everything in the world seems to be placed in reference to him or to her. It once seemed a revolutionary way to write, and Robert Lowell, who was its principal flag bearer, was highly celebrated for doing it.

"At the Train Station in Pamplona" is an example of an altogether different manner of poetry writing: the writing of impersonal observation. You've undoubtedly seen movies in which a nameless spy, or a private detective, sits in a hotel lobby and peers over the top of a newspaper at someone across the room, mentally taking notes. The spy's job is (1) to record what he sees, (2) to avoid calling attention to himself, (3) to draw conclusions from his observations, and (4) to pass all this along to the person who hired him. In "At the Train Station in Pamplona," David Ray is our spy, watching the couple, drawing conclusions based upon their behavior.

Beginning writers, looking for subjects, are frequently advised to write about what they know, and since they know themselves better than anything else, they write about themselves. If they can do this in an interesting and engaging manner, they may enjoy some measure of success. But what about writing about things other than ourselves? There's no end to the possibilities.

Because we've become so used to confessional poetry, writing a poem in which the "I" does not appear even once seems revolutionary. But in the instance of David Ray's poem he is being counterrevolutionary, writing an antithesis to the more popular "I" poem that has been the popular model for half a century.

The manner of the spy in the hotel lobby is to observe closely, to look into the shadows, as it were, and to let the details reveal things to the reader. In Ray's poem the observer notices that the man's hands are in his pockets, suggesting that he may be guarding himself against reaching out to the woman. The woman fiddles with her umbrella, trying to keep herself under control. Notice that nowhere in this poem does the poet step to center stage and stand in the way of what he has interested us in, the nameless couple, whose behavior, as deftly described, reveals so much about themselves.

Here's another example, of something witnessed, by David Allan Evans.

They live alone
together,

she with her wide hind
and bird face,
he with his hung belly
and crewcut.

They never talk
but keep busy.

Today they are
washing windows
(each window together)
she on the inside,
he on the outside.
He squirts Windex
at her face,
she squirts Windex
at his face.

Now they are waving
to each other
with rags,

not smiling.

Notice how well this little poem succeeds in telling us about the relationship between these two people simply by setting down the specifics of how they behave toward each other. Evans doesn't feel called upon to step to center stage and offer his general observations about life, about the virtues of cleaning windows. What he contributes by offering us this poem is a picture of two unique people whom we will never ourselves encounter or be privileged to observe and learn from. We learn from the detail.

Detail. There's a word, both noun and verb, to tack up over your writing desk with your other reminders. Paying attention to even the smallest events can sometimes yield a poem:

At the zenith
of rolling up the window shade
there's a falling into place,
a soft snap
when the winding mechanism
catches hold,
pawl in ratchet,
and the taut pull-string
loosens in your hand
so you can let go,
not just to start the morning,
but to put the last darkness
of the room away—
the night itself
no more than a star map
covering a wall
an hour in science class,
then rolled up somewhere
and forgotten.

This poem by Jane O. Wayne pays attention to something that most of us are familiar with, the little snap when a window shade locks, but which most of us might overlook as being insignificant, not worthy of our time. Yet Wayne, by paying close and careful attention, makes a gift of it to us.

Several years ago I spent some time in a shopping mall, making myself really look at what was before me, sitting on a bench with my notebook or just wandering around on Poetry Patrol. Here's something I observed in a department store:

◈ COSMETICS DEPARTMENT

A fragrance heavy as dust, and two young women
motionless as mannequins, dressed in black.

The white moth of timelessness flutters about them,
unable to leave the cool light of their faces.

One holds the other's head in her hands
like a mirror. The other leans into the long fingers

knowing how heavy her beauty is. Eye to eye,
breath into breath, they lean as if frozen forever:

a white cup with two lithe figures painted in black
and the warm wine brimming.

It's a kind of travel writing, isn't it, even when your travels take you only as far as the shopping mall. Elizabeth Bishop, a master of detail and description, called one of her books *Questions of Travel*, another *Geography III*. Those titles acknowledge her debt to the tradition of telling readers where you've been and what you've seen. Bishop's poem "The Moose," from *Geography III*, is much too long to include here, but I recommend you take a look at it (I'd like to nudge you toward the library whenever I can!). In nearly every line of the 168-line poem, there is a concrete detail. A good exercise is to take a poem like "The Moose" and type it out. This helps you notice how it's put together.

Fortunately, David Ray and others are still out making a record of things they observe and keeping themselves out of the picture. Here's Robert Bly again, with another prose poem:

▪▷ THE DEAD SEAL NEAR MCCLURE'S BEACH

I.

Walking north toward the point, I came on a dead seal. From a few feet away, he looks like a brown log. The body is on its back, dead only a few hours. I stand and look at him. There's a quiver in the dead flesh. My God he is still alive. A shock goes through me, as if a wall of my room had fallen away.

His head is arched back, the small eyes closed, the whiskers sometimes rise and fall. He is dying. This is the oil. Here on its back is the oil that heats our houses so efficiently. Wind blows fine sand back toward the ocean. The flipper near me lies folded over the stomach, looking like an unfinished arm, lightly glazed with sand at the edges. The other flipper lies half underneath. The seal's skin looks like an old overcoat, scratched here and there, by sharp mussel-shells maybe. . . .

I reach out and touch him. Suddenly he rears up, turns over, gives three cries. Awaark! Awaark! Awaark!—like the cries from Christmas toys. He lunges toward me. I am terrified and leap back, although I know there can be no teeth in that jaw. He starts flopping toward the sea. But he falls over, on his face. He does not want to go back to the sea. He looks up at the sky, and he looks like an old lady who has lost her hair.

He puts his chin back on the sand, rearranges his flippers, and waits for me to go. I go.

2.

Today I go back to say goodbye; he's dead now. But he's not—he's a quarter mile farther up the shore. Today he is thinner, squatting on his stomach, head out. The ribs show more—each vertebra on the back under the coat is now visible, shiny. He breathes in and out.

He raises himself up, and tucks his flippers under, as if to keep them warm. A wave comes in, touches his nose. He turns and looks at me—the eyes slanted, the crown of the head is like a black leather jacket. He is taking a long time to die. The whiskers white as porcupine quills, the forehead slopes . . . goodbye brother, die in the sound of waves, forgive us if we have killed you, long live your race, your inner-tube race, so uncomfortable on land, so comfortable in the ocean. Be comfortable in death then, where the sand will be out of your nostrils, and you can swim in long loops through the pure death, ducking under as assassinations break above you. You don't want to be touched by me. I climb the cliff and go home the other way.

Notice how this poem pays attention, and how the poet stands back. Had Bly chosen to write like many of his contemporaries, he might have given us something more self-absorbed, like this:

I passed a dying seal and it made me think of my Uncle
Harry, and how deeply it hurt me when he criticized me
for bumping my bike into the back of Mrs. Murphy's legs,
my first little bike, with its training wheels and its red and
white plastic tassels coming out of the handle-grips, and
how I was so scarred by his brutish insensitivity to my need
for freedom of expression that I have never been able to get
on a bicycle again. . . .

In my example, the poet's self-absorption upstages the death of the
seal.

Though I've been advocating for writing from current observation,
training yourself to pay attention can furnish your memory with detail
you can use later. Here's Jared Carter, writing from distant memory,
but notice how much of his recollection of a time and a people is made
vivid by specific detail:

❧ AT THE SIGN-PAINTER'S

Of them all—those laboring men who knew my first name
And called out to me as I watched them coming up the walk;
The ones with birthmarks and missing fingers and red hair,
Who had worked for my grandfather, and now my father;
Who had gone home to wash up and put on a clean shirt;
Who came to the back door Friday evenings for their checks;
Who drove a Ford coupe and had a second wife and three kids
And were headed for town to have a drink and buy groceries—

Of the ones too old too work—in their black shoes laced up
With hooks, and their string ties, who stood on the sidewalk
When we were building something, and asked my father
If he remembered the house-moving business back during
The Depression: how you squirmed through all that dust
And broken glass in the crawl space, nudging ten by twelves
Twenty feet long, and lugged the house-jacks behind you
One at a time, setting them up just right. How you moved
On your back like a crab through darkness, cobwebs

Brushing your face, an iron bar in your hands, a voice
Calling somewhere from outside, asking for a quarter-turn—

Of them all—plumbers, tinners, roofers, well-diggers,
Carpenters, cement finishers with their padded knees—
I liked the sign-painters best: liked being taken there
By my father, following after him, running my fingers
Along the pipe railing, taking his hand as we climbed up
The concrete embankment to their back-street shop looking
Out across the Nickel Plate yard—
                          liked being left to wander
Among piles of fresh pine planks, tables caked and smeared
And stacked with hundreds of bottles and jars leaking color
And fragrance, coffee cans jammed with dried brushes, skylight
Peppered with dead flies, narrow paths that wound among
Signs shrouded with tape and newspaper—all the way back
To the airshaft, the blackened sink, the two-burner hotplate,
Spoons sticking from china mugs, behind the curtain the bed
With its torn army blanket—liked feeling beneath my toes
The wood floors patterned with forgotten colors, soft
To the step, darkened with grime and soot from the trains—

Liked them most of all—those solemn old men with skin
Bleached and faded as their hair, white muslin caps
Speckled with paint, knuckles and fingers faintly dotted—
Liked them for their listening to him about the sign
He wanted painted, for pretending not to notice me watching—
For the wooden rod with its black knob resting lightly
Against the primed surface, for the slow sweep and whisper
Of the brush—liked seeing the ghost letters in pencil
Gradually filling out, fresh and wet and gleaming, words
Forming out of all that darkness, that huge disorder.

I've heard it said that God is in the details, and also that the Devil is in the details. Both of those aphorisms attest to the power that details carry. Jared Carter, using lots of telling detail, has offered us an entire world.

Another interesting way to pay attention is to capture a snatch of interesting conversation, to capture inflection and dialect and even the spirit of what somebody is saying. Here is a delightful little poem by the late Marnie Walsh, from her book *A Taste of the Knife*, in which she ostensibly records a voice:

➻ BESSIE DREAMING BEAR
ROSEBUD, SO. DAK.,1960

we all went to town one day
went to a store
bought you new shoes
red high heels

aint seen you since

In this brief poem, whose subject is, I'd say, the speaker's voice, the red high heels are a detail we might not have expected. They make the poem more real and vivid. It's often an unexpected or unpredictable detail that authenticates a poem.

We are social creatures by nature and almost never tire of eavesdropping on others, of watching their behavior. Because of our natural curiosity, poems in which the author observes other people and records what they have to say have a distinct advantage in being welcomed by readers. Editors, too, respond warmly to poems about human behavior. You can check me on this by looking at any literary magazine. You'll see that most of the poems are about people.

"Duh!" you say. "Of course they're about people! Poems are written by people!" But in practice there are many other possibilities: poems that describe settings and landscapes, poems describing inanimate objects, poems describing animals, insects, birds. And there are many good poems about, say, birds, like the A. R. Ammons poem about the blue jay. Generally, though, poems about people have an advantage when it comes to being engaging to readers.

Let's look at another, by Thea S. Kuticka:

➻ NEWCASTLE BAR & GRILL

Across the street, a second-hand store displayed gold purses
and a man sold Avon after-shave bottles shaped like Model Ts.

He tried to sell one each time I went in,
even though I was too young to buy cologne for a man.

Summer afternoons, the carpenters walked down to the bar
for a drink and to watch my mother in her cork heels

as she tended to the after-five crowd. Her pockets filled with tips,
quarters spilled from her purse when she pulled out her keys,

and dimes sparkled in the gravel that lined our drive,
but we were still poor, and she was still a single woman

impressed by the man who sat at the bar with his red
Camaro parked out front. The cash drawer sang with change

when she gave it a final tap with her hip at the end of her shift.
She plunked a Shirley Temple down at my table with a half smile

reserved for patrons who didn't tip and gave me a handful
of thin mints hugged in foil. I savored the warm chocolate,

watched the gold purses spark across the street as the Camaro's
headlights lifted out of their sockets for the long drive home.

Notice the value of unexpected, *unpredictable* detail, how it lends authenticity to this poem.

If I were to ask each of you in turn to provide, from your imaginations, one or two details from a scene like this one, I'd expect you to come up with the obvious ones: cigarette butts in the ashtrays, a clock over the counter, the smell of grease, the clink of dishes, and so on, and soon, as we added detail upon detail, we would have assembled a kind of Norman Rockwell bar and grill. But it wouldn't feel quite real because we would have built it from the *predictable* details, from our imaginations. There would be little about our imaginary scene to convince the viewer that any of us had ever been in this specific bar and grill. But if one of us dropped in just one *unpredictable* detail, say a cardboard box covered with Christmas paper, sitting on the end of the counter and filled with carburetor parts, the whole scene would gain in authenticity because somebody viewing our assembled scene would think, "Well, those poets must have been there, all right, to have seen that box on the counter."

Kuticka's poem has lots of unpredictable details, and for me, building one upon the other, they lend the poem great authenticity. This poem really sounds like the truth, doesn't it? Would any of us, imagining a scene like this, have thought up the gold purses, the Avon bottles shaped like Model Ts, the mother's cork heels, the dimes in the gravel, and those wonderful socketed headlights on the red Camaro?

When I was beginning to write, Robert Bly once criticized a poem of mine, saying, "You're just making this up." He meant that I'd created the scene and experience from my imagination, sitting in my comfortable chair under my floor lamp. What I'd put there were the predictable things, the kinds of details the imagination finds easily. The imagination makes a lousy realist; it places in its scenes only those things that it prefers to see there. Bly was encouraging me to write from life, to go out and actually experience something and then write about that while its particular and unique detail was fresh in mind.

Bly's own work is chock full of poems rich with authentic, unpredictable detail. When he describes that dying seal on a beach in California we are persuaded by his detailing that he was really present, that he wasn't in rural Minnesota making it up. His prose poems are especially artful in their detailing.

Just keep in mind that it won't be the birthday cake covered with twinkling candles that will make readers feel that you were really at the party, but the bone-handled serving fork with one tine missing and the place where the lace has pulled loose from the hem of the tablecloth.

And while we're speaking about particulars, have you noticed that there is something very attractive about knowing the specific names of things? Adam had the privilege of starting the human race, which you may or may not see as a mistake, depending on whether you're a human being or a spotted owl. But what must have been just as much fun, if not more, was getting to put the names on everything he came upon, furry, feathered, or covered with moss, or not covered at all, as it happened with Eve.

Since then, nearly all of us take pleasure and even feel a little power in knowing the specific names of things. Donald Hall, in his wonderful poem "Names of Horses," describes the lives and deaths of draft horses, and at the very end, lists the horses he's known by their names:

Roger, Mackerel, Lady Ghost. Just by doing that, he makes the lost horses especially luminous and unforgettable.

In the following poem by Gerald Costanzo, we can sense his pleasure in being able, after many years of being away, to recite the names of the roses in his native place, to know that the trees are Douglas firs, to know that the city he left is intact, with its names and its landmarks, after long absence. And the presence of these specific names in the poem authenticates the experience for us.

➡ WASHINGTON PARK

I went walking in the Rose Gardens.
It was about to rain, but the roses
were beginning to bloom. The Olympiads,

some Shreveports, and the Royal
Sunsets. This was in the beautiful
city I had taken away from myself

years before, and now I was giving it back.
I walked over the Rosaria tiles
and found Queen Joan of 1945. I sat

on the hillside overlooking the reservoir
and studied the Willamette and the Douglas
firs. I learned the traffic

and the new highrises as the rain
came down.
                    This leaving and returning,

years of anger and forgiveness,
the attempts to forgive one's self—
it's everybody's story,

and I was sitting there
filling up again with the part of it
that was mine.

If he were just dreaming up this poem, Costanzo could have looked the names up in a book. But by mentioning walking across the *Rosaria* tiles he adds the unexpected information that really makes us believe he was on the scene in the park.

Artful use of detail is not the central theme of this poem, of course. The detail merely sets the stage. The main theme is, as he says,

> This leaving and returning,

and how a place and a life once rejected can be taken back into the heart.

Here's a translation, from the Russian, by Jane Kenyon. It's one of Anna Akmahtova's untitled poems, written in 1917. Notice the detailing:

> We walk along the hard crest of the snowdrift
> toward my white, mysterious house,
> both of us so quiet,
> keeping the silence as we go along.
> And sweeter even than the singing of songs
> is this dream, now becoming real:
> the swaying of branches brushed aside
> and the faint ringing of your spurs.

Much of the magic of this little poem comes from very deft handling of the auditory sense. Notice how the ringing of the spurs, the only sound, at the very end of the poem, is showcased by the meticulous enforcement of silences elsewhere. Despite the fact that the couple is walking across hard snow, and we might expect to hear footsteps, there is no noise in the first line, and then none in the second, and so on. Throughout the poem the *absence* of sound is heightened and used. She even underlines the absence of noise by "both of us so quiet, / keeping the silence as we go along." And then that silence is heightened even further by "And sweeter *even* than the singing of songs" (emphasis mine) so that when we finally come to the "faint ringing of your spurs" that ringing carries so much.

Here's another good example of unpredictable detail from Charles Baxter's 2003 novel, *Saul and Patsy*, published by Pantheon. Early in the story, Patsy asks her husband, Saul, to go down to the cellar of their rented house to dispose of a dead mouse in a trap: "He stood up, shaking the letters on the Scrabble board, and clomped in his white socks to the kitchen, where the flashlight was stuck to the refrigerator with a magnet that was so weak that the flashlight kept sliding down to the floor, though it was only halfway there now. 'I didn't say you had to do it *instantly*,' Patsy shouted. 'This very minute. You could wait until the game is over.'"

That flashlight with its weak magnet is the authenticating detail in this scene, completely unpredictable. It makes the scene real.

I'll close this chapter with a poem by Donald Finkle, based upon paying attention to something. The poem is triggered by a momentary event, a sonic boom, and the poet pays attention to the specifics that surround that event. And, returning momentarily to what I said about first impressions, notice how easily he draws us in, using very ordinary, conversational language. Once we are safely aboard, the poem begins to lift off:

⇒ SONIC BOOM

Nothing has happened, nothing has been broken,
everything is still in place, including yourself;
even now the juice of alarm begins to settle:
the bomber drags away her diminishing roar.
Nothing has happened; this was practice,
you are free to return. If there is a day
to come when you will be called out
to answer for somebody else's doings, this is not it.

Yet what is this delicate balance, that it shall not
be shaken? On the bookcase the figurine teeters;
which of its two thousand years gives it the right
to withstand one blow of the wind? Somewhere over
the plains an angel gathered enough speed
to outrun even the sound of her own voice.
In consequence, for miles around the night
exploded with the violence of her escape.
Yet she has not escaped. Behind her
and her ghostly silence, wherever she goes,
she drags like a harrow her unsettling past.

CHAPTER TEN

Controlling Effects
through Careful Choices

THE SHADOWS CAST BY NOUNS

Reading, you turn a page to a poem you haven't encountered before. Think of this poem as a bare table, well lighted, with darkness all around. It's your table; each reader has his or her own. As you begin to read, to follow the poem word by word, the poet sets one thing after another on your table. With every noun the poet sets out, there is something for you to envision, first a chicken, then a washing machine, then a half-melted candle in the neck of a jug. Verbs move these things around, defining their actions.

But first I want to call your attention to the nouns and the way you can control the associations they offer up.

Let's go back to the beginning. Say a poet writes, "She had eyes like a chicken." Presto! A chicken pops into your mind, and whatever personal associations you as a reader have with chickens arrive as well. Maybe one of your many associations is the vivid memory of an ill-tempered red rooster that bit your leg when you were a child. He had fierce yellow eyes. How you hated to walk through that chicken yard when he was out there waiting for you! But there were also those pleasant white hens your grandmother kept, warm, pillowlike creatures that never objected when you reached for an egg. Their eyes seemed less hostile. Whatever your personal experiences with chickens, and there may have been many, they all gather around the word "chicken." On the table of the poem, once the word "chicken" appears, you have dozens of chickens, some mean, some friendly, some red, some black, some you read about in books, maybe one that got killed by a neighbor's dog and a delectable one you ate at your Great Aunt Mildred's, pan-fried with dumplings and gravy, followed by a big wedge of strawberry-rhubarb pie with ice cream.

Then comes the washing machine. The poet goes on, "and a heart like a washing machine." Presto! In your mind a washing machine starts rocking and gurgling under a heavy load of your grandmother's winter bedding. It's the first day of spring, kites flying, a robin's egg in your pocket. Suddenly, though, in your mind there's another washing machine. This second one is broken, its motor burned out, a dead machine pushed back into a dank cellar corner. This last one smells like mildew and the first one like Rinso Blue.

I needn't go on and on. You know what I'm talking about. We've already got a lot of chickens and a couple of washing machines on the table. Then there's that candle in the jug to deal with. That candle may be lit in one of your associations and snuffed out in another. Maybe with one there is the sound of Ravi Shankar playing the sitar and the smell of patchouli oil. Maybe in another there is a cold, dark room with a wick just then pinched out and a burning spot between your thumb and index finger. Maybe there's that candle that accidentally lit your neighbors' bedroom curtains on fire and burned down their house.

This process of collecting associations goes on, stirred by noun after noun, shifted by verbs. After thirty or forty lines, the table gets pretty full. Though some private associations may get crowded out as they accumulate, there is a kind of lingering half-life or after-image for almost everything named. We'll call it a noun shadow. By the end of the poem, that candle, just a noun dropped into a metaphor like "My love for her was like a candle burning" may have been pushed off toward the edge of your awareness as a reader, but there still may be a wisp of smoke from a tiny red coal at the tip of its wick.

Most poets wish to achieve some definite effect upon their readers, and a reader's collective associations with words have a lot to do with that effect. How can a poet attempt to control it? There are many ways, of course, including form and rhythm and tone and vocabulary, but one important way is to try to limit the variety of associations a reader may have.

You can do this with modifiers, specifically adjectives.

WORKING WITH ADJECTIVES AND ADVERBS

You may have been taught in writing courses that adjectives make for weak writing, and it's true that an overabundance of adjectives can sap the strength of a poem or essay or story, but they can be extremely useful in limiting the number of associations that arise in a reader's mind. If a poet writes, "She had eyes like a chicken, cold and unblinking and glassy," he or she immediately steers the reader's associations away from those placid laying hens toward a more dangerous chicken, one that shows a little of the reptile in its distant ancestry. And then there's the woman, with eyes as reptilian as the chicken's eyes. By selecting adjectives, a poet can reduce the number of chickens on the reader's table from a dozen to maybe one or two. Add just one modifier and "She had a heart like a *broken* washing machine" immediately excludes that pleasant gurgling, sloshing machine on your grandmother's side porch. And adjectives that specify number are especially useful. It is much easier for a reader to envision "three chickens" than "chickens." *Chickens* is murky; there could be three or three hundred.

Keep in mind that every noun in a poem evokes a complex of associations in your reader's mind. Never put in a noun without thinking about its possible associations. Then use adjectives sparingly and with precision to exclude the associations you don't want, and to make the remaining things on the table work toward the effect you want to achieve. This isn't a license to use strings of adjectives, of course, because they do make writing flabby. If you think about it—and you ought to think about every word in the poems you write—there is probably one good adjective that will push aside most of the superfluous associations. That's the one you're looking for.

You've undoubtedly been told that writing with nouns and verbs makes for a strong and forceful poetry, and that adjectives and adverbs tend to weaken your writing. Part of that weakness comes from using modifiers when they just aren't needed. It would be a rare instance in which you'd need to write "white snow" because in almost everybody's mind snow is white. Though leaves are green in spring and summer, and yellow and red in autumn, you rarely need to write "green leaves" because most of us immediately think of green leaves when the word "leaves" appears. The same is true of "blue sky" or "red apple." And so on. *Try to give your reader credit for being able to supply at least some of the description.* And as to adverbs, if you use the verb "creep" there's no point, is there, in writing "creep slowly?" Creeping is slow.

In addition to the uses mentioned above, adjectives are helpful, of course, when the noun they modify doesn't adequately describe itself. A noun like "baseball" describes itself perfectly because we all know what size a baseball is and what it feels and looks like. To add an adjective is just overkill: "He threw the hard baseball." Or worse, "He threw the hard white baseball."

Adverbs can usually be avoided by finding a more specific and accurate verb. You don't need to write "She walked very slowly and warily up the stair," if "She crept up the stair" will accurately describe the action.

WRITING WITH VERBS

Here is a poem by Ted Genoways. Notice how his use of verbs and nouns puts a lot of action into his poem:

☞ NIGHT TRAIN
THEODORE THOMPSON GENOWAYS, DECEMBER 28, 1916

He stirs before dawn, tucks a lantern in his pack,
and leans out into the cold. Half-dark, chimney smoke
feathers and molts, circling the frozen window glass,

fading across drifted fields. He wades through snowbanks,
windblown to the eaves of an abandoned milk shed,
and across the barnyard, where leaf-bare cottonwoods

and evergreens stretch from the farm to deeper woods.
His skates curl like a promise in his canvas pack.
At the river's edge, he builds a small fire and sheds

his overshoes, while gusts send a thick rope of smoke
and cherry sparks, swirling toward the distant bank.
Late last August, he honed his father's reading glass

on a knot of bluestem and dried cobs, till the glass
shimmered, grass curled and burned. He piled on scrubwood,
then whole logs. Together, the boys walked the ditch bank,

touching torches to each row, but Ted trailed the pack,
blinking as his brothers—one by one—passed into smoke.
He kindles his lantern. The little light it sheds

casts his legs in wide shadow, down the watershed
and across the river, stretched below like frosted glass.
He buckles his skates, watching the gray thread of smoke

from his chimney stitch across the sheltering woods,
firs straight and green as soldiers. He shoulders his pack
and takes a long, gliding step from the near bank,

buoyed on a scalpel blade of steel, toward the bank
on the far shore. For a moment, the valley—washed
in moonlight, the sky-blue glow of ice and snowpack—

speeds and scrolls by him, as if passing through the glass
of a Pullman car. Boys fresh from the backwoods
crowded the platform that summer morning, coal smoke

dotting girl's dresses with soot as the train left, smoke
clinging to their tear-streaked cheeks. He curls on the bank
under the bridge, waiting for thunder from the woods

to jar ashes, bitternut, bur-oak till they shed
their brittle leaves. Its hiss echoes like breaking glass
or a snake in tall reeds. He braces for impact.

From the bone-black woods, the night train rockets past, packed
with sleeping recruits. It banks through the plume of smoke
it sheds like a skin and slithers on tracks of glass.

   Let's look at this poem, a sestina that uses three-line stanzas rather
than six-line, simply as the description of a series of actions. As you
might expect, since verbs create action, the verbs do most of the heavy
hauling. If you make a list—*stirs, tucks, leans, feathers, molts, circling,
fading, wades*, etc.—you can see how numerous the verbs are, and how
they draw the poem forward. And where are the adverbs? Well, a poet
doesn't need to write "softly stirs," "neatly tucks," and so on. We know
the actions those verbs describe: to tuck in something is to tuck it

neatly. If you wanted to convey a sloppy tucking, you'd choose another verb, like "jam" or "stuff."

As to his use of adjectives, they are there only when necessary: "stretched below like frosted glass" uses "frosted" because there isn't a one-word noun for frosted glass, and Genoways wants to describe the frozen river quickly and efficiently.

Beyond the masterful use of nouns and verbs, you might notice the form, which is so subtle as to be unobtrusive but which adds a subtle music as the end words rhyme, chime, and repeat, weaving in and out of the action.

TRUSTING YOUR READER TO HELP YOU ALONG

I've talked about how you can trust your reader to supply a portion of every setting, based upon his or her experience. You may not need all the modifiers, all the explanations. For example, were you to write, "I climbed very slowly into the strong branches of the tree and looked out over the green field of corn," I would respond, "Well, is it expected that someone might climb quickly into a tree? Climbing a tree is by its nature slow. And as to the tree itself, what do you climb into but its branches, and don't you choose the strong branches because they support your weight? And, is your first thought of a field of corn anything but of a field of green?"

So the adequate sentence is shorter and more energetic, written with strong nouns and verbs, not sagging with modifiers: "I climbed into the tree and looked out over the corn." We readers supply all the other stuff.

I wrote this little exercise for this book, to illustrate the phenomenon of the reader supplying much of the literary experience of a poem. Or of an essay or story, for that matter:

➡ MORNING GLORIES

We share so much. When I write lattice,
I count on you seeing the flimsy slats
tacked into squares and painted white,

like a French door propped in a garden
with a blue condensed from many skies
pressed up against the panes. I count on

you knowing that remarkable blue,
shaped into the fluted amplifying horns
of Edison cylinder record players.

What? Come on, you know exactly
what I'm talking about. I didn't need
to describe them like that, but I like to

hover a little over my words, dabbling
the end of my finger in the white throats
of those _____. You fill it in.

I could go on, but all I really needed to do
was to give you the name in the title.
I knew you'd put in the rest, maybe

the smell of a straw hat hot from the sun;
that's just a suggestion. You know exactly
what else goes into a picture like this

to make it seem as if you saw it first,
how a person can lean on the warm
hoe handle of a poem, dreaming,

making a little more out of the world
than was there just a moment before.
I'm just the guy who gets it started.

GETTING THE MOST OUT OF LINE ENDINGS

From teaching I've learned that beginning poets very often have diffi-
culty deciding where to end their lines, and all too often do it arbitrarily.

A line ending is a force in a poem, much like a punctuation mark.
That white space out there on the right is an opportunity, and you ought
to take advantage of it.

Here's the kind of writing I see too much of:

Mother and I went down to the shoe
store and she took along her white
purse so she could get a pair of
shoes to match.

When I was talking about transparency in writing, about avoiding things that will cause your reader to lose touch with the poetry and draw back to ponder what you're doing, I might have included something about line endings like these. See how unnatural they feel, how much they ask of a reader? What would be wrong with using more logical units of speech, like:

> Mother and I went down to the shoe store
> and she took along her white purse
> so she could get a pair of shoes to match.

I don't think there's any poetry in either one of these examples, by the way, but I want to make a point: the closer your writing gets to the pacing of conversational speech, the less it's likely to call attention to itself.

While you're reading the work of other poets, pay attention to the way in which they end their lines. Notice how often they use that white space on the right to good effect.

One interesting way is to try a strong verb, something like this:

> John ran to the end of the line and leapt
> into space

The substance of that verb, the leaping, seems to hang out there in space for just an instant, the way Wile E. Coyote does when he runs off the edge of the cliff, before he makes the mistake of looking down. See how different the effect would be to break the line on the article?

> John ran to the end of the line and
> leapt into space

In this latter instance, the conjunction, followed by the white space, provides a little suspense: What is John going to do? Well, after that pause we learn he's going to leap.

In Mary Oliver's "Little Summer Poem Touching the Subject of Faith," notice how much she gets out of the space after "hear":

> Every summer
> I listen and look

under the sun's brass and even
into the moonlight but I can't hear

anything, I can't see anything . . .

Here's an example of a line ending that causes a reader to have to
stop for an instant, back up and think:

We didn't know what to do about her birth
marks all over her back.

We read "birth" first as a noun, then have to adjust for its use as
an adjective modifying "marks." Compounding the problem, "marks"
can be read as both noun and verb. We have to pause, if only for an
instant, to puzzle out the usage. All it would take to correct this would
be to put "marks" on the same line with "birth." Little things like this
make a considerable difference.

THE POPULAR PRESENT TENSE

Let's say that eons from now some archeologist unearths a private
library with a couple of thousand volumes of twentieth-century poetry.
By a miracle, the books are still readable, though crumbling. With her
graduate assistants she carefully studies the books to see what can be
discerned about our ancient, vanished society. After assembling her
notes, she publishes an article that begins, "In America in the late
twentieth century, nearly everybody wrote exclusively in the present
tense. Even little stories about past experiences, which one might
expect to be told in past tense, were told in present." And so on.

Has it ever struck you as peculiar that, even though we almost always
talk about our lives in the past tense, so much contemporary poetry is
written in the present, as if that were one of the rules? Somehow poets
have gotten the idea that to write in present tense is really cool, that it's
the way it's supposed to be done. I've heard it said in its defense that the
present tense makes the experience of a poem more immediate, and
I suppose there's something to be said for that. But if, as Baudelaire
thought, art holds up a mirror to life, why aren't more poems written
in past tense, which is the natural way we tell another person about
something that's happened to us?

As poets you'll need to make decisions about tenses, and I don't expect you to abandon the present tense. But just because it is the current convention doesn't mean you are limited to it. There is a naturalness to be gained by telling stories in past tense. That's how we usually tell them: "I pulled into the gas station this morning, and there was a girl in pigtails filling the tires on her bike . . ."

SELECTING THE VERY BEST WORD

When writing even a very brief poem, you have hundreds of decisions to make—choices of words, of syntax, of punctuation, of rhythm, and so on. A poem is a machine of language designed to accomplish something. Whatever the poet hopes to accomplish, the work of writing the poem can't be hurried. Every word must be selected for its appropriateness to the task at hand, just as each part of a machine must contribute to its effectiveness. Each choice the poet makes must bring the poem a little closer to its potential. It is impossible to achieve perfection, but any poem will be more effective if it falls just a little short of perfection rather than a long way short.

Several years ago I developed the following exercise to use in poetry workshops to emphasize how important it can be to get just the right word. It is based on a poem by the late Lorine Niedecker, who wrote many fine short poems.

You'll see that I've left out one of the words. The task is to choose a word that brings the most to the poem, that enlivens or animates it, that, we might say, carries a big charge, a word that is not just a verb but that amplifies or expands upon what the poem seems to be aiming for. You may turn a noun into a verb if you wish. Don't be afraid to have fun. Writing poetry is a kind of play.

⇒ POPCORN-CAN COVER

Popcorn-can cover
screwed to the wall
over a hole
so the cold
can't _____ in.

Here are some typical words that students have offered when I've used this exercise: "creep," "squeeze," "sneak," "reach," "seep," "rush," "jump," and "pop." You may have come up with others. I've held workshops in which students came up with a dozen or more.

Now, can you think of one word that might include more than one of these others, that is, that might include some of the characteristics of the others? Is there a word whose meaning contains, say, all these: "creep," "squeeze," and "sneak?"

Well, yes. Here's Niedecker's poem as she published it:

◆ POPCORN-CAN COVER

Popcorn-can cover
screwed to the wall
over a hole
so the cold
can't mouse in.

Niedecker chose the word "mouse," which contains a lot of creepiness, and some squeezing through things, and sneaking around. It is a word that in effect contains all sorts of other words. By choosing the strongest word, the word that contains the most, your poem can gain in its effect on the reader.

Here is another example of using just the right word. I probably won't need to point it out to you. The whole poem, by Robert Francis, hinges upon it.

◆ SHEEP

From where I stand the sheep stand still
As stones against the stony hill.

The stones are gray
And so are they.

And both are weatherworn and round,
Leading the eye back to the ground.

Two mingled flocks—
The sheep, the rocks.

And still no sheep stirs from its place
Or lifts its Babylonian face.

That remarkable word, Babylonian, brings all sorts of things into this poem, doesn't it—sculpture, history, mutability—and when it appears the entire poem suddenly lifts.

Here's another, by David Allan Evans:

⊷ THE STORY OF LAVA

Every time I smell Lava soap it is 1948.
My father is bending over a long sink in the
pressroom of The Sioux City Journal at 5 a.m.,
his grey long-underwear peeled down over his
white belly, a thin bar of Lava tumbling over
and over slowly in his ink-stained hands.
The morning news has passed through his hands
out into the morning streets into the hands
of sleepy boys who fold it a certain way and
fling it on porches and steps, but that is not
my story. Lava is my story and the morning
news that Lava can't rub off. It is my father
bending over a sink, a thin bar of Lava tumbling
over and over and over slowly in his cloudy hands.

Notice how that one word, "cloudy," in the last line, makes all the difference, suggesting the father's mutability.

A good example of how much trouble a single word can cause is when somebody writes something like, *With his left hand, he touched the corner of his mouth.* By specifying the left hand, the writer has risked making the reader wonder what the character is doing with his other hand. The writer probably doesn't want a reader to pause in the middle of things to wonder about that. By omitting *left*, the problem could be avoided.

Sometimes, though, the addition of a specific modifier like *left* can help the reader visualize a scene. It is almost always better to write *three dogs were crossing the road* than *some dogs were crossing the road*. It's easier to "see" three dogs than "some."

Let's look at another example, by Jonathan Greene:

➡ VESTIGE

Mother had died
that morning.

In the closet
a chalice of her last night's urine,
now numinous relic.

And yet, without fanfare,
what is to be done
but empty it into the weeds. . . .

Most of us who relish words—as poets do—tend to almost uncon-
sciously adjust our vocabulary and the pitch of our rhetoric to suit
the occasion, playing with the language for the sheer pleasure of it,
and this poem is a good example of using such playfulness to good
effect.

The words of the first stanza and the first line of the second are
completely matter-of-fact, flatly reporting the death and the location of
the beaker of urine. This flatness of tone and vocabulary is of course the
style of fact, useful here to drive home the unadorned truth of the death
and establish a ground upon which the rest of the poem will build.

The second and third lines of the second stanza make light of
the way in which, when grieving, we elevate the status of even the
homeliest things left behind by the dead. Someone in your family
holds up some shabby scrap and says, "Oh, dear, here is her favorite
brassiere!" Because in grief our responses are often hypersensitive and
exaggerated, Greene uses the words *chalice*, *numinous*, and *relic*, which
gild the lily in a humorous but at the same time poignant way. After all,
this is a death we're talking about, being treated lightly, perhaps as a
means of defending against grief.

The last stanza brings us back to the practical, taking us away from
the momentary exaggeration, the "fanfare," and setting us back on
course. This death, with its ceremonies, is past us now, and it's time to
move on. The urine gets poured into the weeds. Notice the big contrast
in tone between "numinous relic" and "empty it into the weeds."

It's quite a complex little poem, humorous, yes, but much more than that. It shows the transit or course of human grief, from fact, to exaggerated response, to practicality and moving on. And accomplished largely through specific word and tone choices, coupled to an engaging anecdote.

CHAPTER ELEVEN

Fine-Tuning Metaphors and Similes

A figure of speech is not just an ornament that a poet attaches to a poem the way people put glass balls on Christmas trees. A metaphor or simile should be used to clarify a poem. For this chapter I've tried to choose examples that show this clarifying activity.

> There was a pond on which we learned to skate,
> Where the blades flashed like sabres, and the ice,
> Scored and carved as an old dinner plate,
> Lay locked within its shores as in a vise.

This is the first stanza of "A Skater's Waltz" by Gray Burr. I want to use it as an example of how the use of simile differs from the use of metaphor.

There are, as you see, three similes: blades like sabres, lake as dinner plate, and lake as something in a vice. None of these is directly related to another, yet the description of the lake feels natural and doesn't seem to call undue attention to itself. That's because speech using similes is generally more relaxed and easygoing than speech using metaphors. Metaphors set up precise identities between the two halves of a comparison, while similes are less demanding.

You may have noticed how we throw similes around as if they meant nothing. Listen in on conversations and you'll hear people say, "That birthday cake was like . . . well, it was like . . . it was like a . . ." and so on until the other half of the comparison occurs to the speaker. And the other half may not be a very precise choice.

Now look at the stanza as I've rewritten it, using metaphor:

There was a pond on which we learned to skate,
Where the blades were flashing sabres, and the ice
was an old dinner plate, scored and carved,
locked within its shores by a vise.

I had to ruin the rhyme between lines 1 and 3, which diminishes the effect of the stanza, but my point is that the use of metaphor calls attention to itself in this revision because now the comparisons *work against each other*. Where we originally had three things that *casually* resembled three other things, now we have three things that *are* three other things. The most obvious problem, one of logic, is that the old dinner plate is locked in a vise, and what, we might ask ourselves, is a plate doing in a vise? And to fit into a vice the plate would have to be on edge; a lake is nothing like a plate on edge.

When you want your poem to feel more casual and conversational, more like everyday speech, and you raise a comparison, a simile can sometimes be a better choice than a metaphor. But keep in mind that most similes lack the authority that metaphors convey. Metaphors almost always sound more forceful, more confident, which in turn makes the poem's presence more confident and forceful. The choice, like the thousand other choices you'll make in writing a poem, is yours.

A metaphor is emphatic: *a boat of cupped hands*. Metaphor conveys a confidence and certainty that in turn characterizes the speaker, and of course the character of the speaker affects the way in which the poem affects the reader. Is your imaginary reader likely to be more attracted to a confident speaker or one less confident? Which works best for the particular poem you're writing? Compared with a metaphor, a simile is always less sure of itself. It presents a different, less certain speaker: *cupped hands are like a boat*. You can imagine such a speaker saying something like, "Cupped hands are like . . . well, they're like . . . you know, they're sort of like . . . a boat."

That doesn't mean that metaphor is superior to simile, or vice versa, but that each has its own "personality."

One of my friends was listening to a tape of a World War I veteran on public radio. The speaker had been at the Battle of the Somme, and was talking about the thousands of corpses in the no-man's land between the lines. He said there were millions of bluebottle flies that swarmed over the corpses for weeks, laying eggs in the decaying flesh. Then later, he said, the eggs hatched, and "maggots came out like froth." Horrible as this scene is, it provides an example of the effectiveness of a simile as opposed to a metaphor. As I've suggested, there is something very human about simile. It can reflect our inadequacies or uncertainties. We say, those maggots were like, well, they were like, sort of like a . . . froth. That indefiniteness or lack of complete confidence in what is being said is very humble and human and common. This statement, if expressed with the absolute confidence of metaphor—the eggs hatched and a froth of maggots came out—would, I think, be a little too confident and, I think, less effective in expressing the wonder and horror.

Here's a poem by Mary Oliver:

⇒ BREAKAGE

> I go down to the edge of the sea.
> How everything shines in the morning light!
> The cusp of the whelk,
> the broken cupboard of the clam,
> the opened, blue mussels,
> moon snails, pale pink and barnacle scarred—
> and nothing at all whole or shut, but tattered, split,
> dropped by the gulls onto the gray rocks and all the
>   moisture gone.
> It's like a schoolhouse
> of little words,
> thousands of words.
> First you figure out what each one means by itself,
> the jingle, the periwinkle, the scallop
>   full of moonlight.
>
> Then you begin, slowly, to read the whole story.

"Breakage" provides an example of the deft use of simile. "It's like a schoolhouse / of little words," Oliver writes, not "It's a school-house . . ." A metaphor, a complete identification of the debris on the beach with a schoolhouse, just won't hold up under scrutiny. By using "like," the poet casts a looser net—a simile—over the things on the beach, and we readers are more likely to accept it without question.

There are also instances in which poets decide whether to use a simile or a metaphor based upon clarity. Here is an early draft of a poem of mine that eventually appeared in the *Hudson Review*.

➻ THE POSSIBLE LIVES

> There were once so many I might choose among,
> a warehouse of coats and shoes, and all my size.
> Walking the streets I imagined myself in every house,
> happy with whichever woman might be living there.
> How might it be to be at home among the odors
> of a hundred different lives, opening the curtains
> each morning to a different view? Now I know
> that this life I have is the only one I have ever had
> or will ever be given, a cord of braided dreams
> that I follow, hand over hand, into the distance.

When I looked at this poem after giving it a few days' rest, I noticed that it wasn't clear just what I was talking about in the first two lines. Because I'd used "a warehouse of coats and shoes" it could be read literally, that I was choosing among coats and shoes and not possible lives, which I meant to be addressing. So I made the change to a simile and made it clear what I was trying to say:

> There were once so many I might choose among,
> like a warehouse of coats and shoes, and all my size.

There are lots of marvelous poems that are built upon a single expanded comparison, either simile or metaphor. May Swenson's poem "The Even Sea" is a good example:

➻ THE EVEN SEA

> Meekly the sea
> now plods to shore:
> white-faced cattle used to their yard,
> the waves, with weary knees,
> come back from bouldered hills
> of high water,

> where all the gray, rough day they seethed like bulls,
> till the wind laid down its goads
> at shift of tide, and sundown
> gentled them, with lowered necks
> they amble up the beach
> as to their stalls.

This metaphor has two halves, or sides: the sea and the cattle. The sea with its waves is the subject of the poem, and its comparison to a herd of cattle is the imaginative means by which the subject is made more interesting and memorable.

To make such a comparison have its strongest effect, the poet must work only with those aspects of each half that find some kind of reflection in the other half.

Note that Swenson's comparison—the sea to a herd of cows—is strictly visual; the poet uses no sounds, no odors, no tastes, no tactile impressions. This is because though cattle low and bellow, the sea does not. And the sea makes a different noise that can't be reasonably compared with any sound a cow might make. In addition, the sea is wet but the cattle are not. And cattle smell one way, the sea another. So Swenson plays upon the ways the two sides are *alike* and is careful not to include how they *differ*. Any detail on one side of the metaphor that could not be mirrored in the other side might have broken the back of the poem. For example:

> Meekly the sea
> now plods to shore
> with manure on its hooves

or

> Meekly the sea
> now plods to shore,
> mooing with longing

Through the details you choose for your metaphors you tell the reader a little about yourself (or about the speaker of the poem, if you are writing from the point of view of someone other than yourself). And if you characterize your speaker through the use of figures of speech and other word choices, you have no need to make expository statements about that speaker's background. No need for May Swenson to begin her poem:

> I grew up on a farm
> and my father had cattle.
> Meekly the sea
> now plods to shore:
> white-faced cattle used to their yard,
> the waves, with weary knees,
> come back from bouldered hills
> of high water.

Metaphor-centered poems, that is, poems that begin with a comparison and are expanded from there, like that of Swenson, are of a type I have explored in my own work over and over:

⟜ STUDENT

> The green shell of his backpack makes him lean
> into wave after wave of responsibility,
> and he swings his stiff arms and cupped hands,
>
> paddling ahead. He has extended his neck
> to its full length, and his chin, hard as a beak,
> breaks the cold surf. He's got his baseball cap on
>
> backward as up he crawls, out of the froth
> of a hangover and onto the sand of the future,
> and lumbers, heavy with hope, into the library.

"Student" is not a notable poem by any means, but a handy example of beginning a poem with a simple comparison, then expanding upon that comparison, being careful not to incorporate detail on one side of the metaphor that can't be mirrored on the other. The "form" of such a poem is the limits to which the comparison can be stretched.

We talk a lot about "ideas" for poems, but to me an idea is a plan, a kind of outline. Building a poem from a comparison is the discovery-in-process of a plan, or perhaps the playful pursuit of an idea. In short, I didn't have any idea what I was doing or where I was going until I started following the trail of my imagination.

I noticed one day that students wearing backpacks looked a little like sea turtles lumbering up onto a beach to lay their eggs, and the poem grew from that initial comparison. Notice how I've tried to use imagery that will both describe a turtle and the student. At one point I step outside this equation to talk about the ball cap, which turtles don't wear, but it did seem to me that a turtle's head looks a little as if it had a ball cap on backward, that is, a cap with no bill in front. I studiously avoided saying things that couldn't work on both sides: I didn't talk about a turtle's diet of seaweed and little sea creatures, nor about the student's Burger King diet. I didn't get into what might be in the backpack because the turtle doesn't carry anything but itself under its shell. And so on. I didn't say that turtles are slimy and cold and scaly because students are not.

Another term for expanding upon a single metaphor is "follow through," meaning that once the comparison is set up you try to extract everything you can from it.

Here is another poem of mine, a much earlier one, built upon a single comparison, with a follow through:

➻ CAMERA

It's an old box camera,
a Brownie, the color and shape
of the battery out of a car,
but smaller, lighter.
All the good times—
the clumsy picnics on the grass,
the new Dodge,
the Easter Sundays—
each with its own clear instant
in the fluid of time,
all these have leaked away,
leaving this shell,
this little battery without a spark.

The first four lines of this poem set up a simple comparison, one that anyone might make. The box camera is described as being the color and shape of a car battery, but smaller and lighter. Simple enough. In classical terminology, the real camera is the "tenor," and the imaginary car battery is the "vehicle." But for our purposes, let's say that the Brownie camera I'm describing is right in front of me and is, therefore, of this world, or worldly, while the imaginary battery is of my imagination, or otherworldly.

Once the simple comparison has been made, the poem spends the next four lines in the worldly side of the comparison, talking about the work that the camera has done in the past. Nothing in these four lines relates to the vehicle, the otherworldly battery. Since the poem is really about the camera, not the battery, the camera gets most of the attention.

In line 9, I begin to braid the tenor and vehicle together, making sure that the details I choose work for both. Note that the word "clear" in this line describes both the quality of light and the clear fluid in the battery.

Line 10 continues this braiding, setting up parallels between the camera and battery: not only do they both have something "clear" about them, they also have something "fluid." The battery has its own clear battery fluid, and the camera's activity is to capture an instant from the clear light flowing through time. Before ever coming upon this poem, the reader has already accepted, I believe, that time is fluid; the poem simply reminds him or her of this.

I go on to imply that for the camera, the clear instants of the new Dodge, the Easter Sundays—those happy human moments—have leaked away over the years. In other words, the camera no longer holds these fluid images, just as an old car battery may have dried up, leaving only a shell—the black box of the camera, the black box of the battery.

At this point, it is important that I try to bring everything together quickly and with enough "snap" that my reader will feel a release from the metaphor. A metaphor is a confining thing, and I have trapped my reader in my comparison and must now release him or her. I try to accomplish this by using a single line:

this little battery without a spark.

Note that I am here straddling the metaphor as I try to rejoin both halves of my association: Batteries have sparks, and the shutter of a camera makes a little spark of light.

The entire poem is one metaphor, one comparison, stretched over several lines from the initial "tenor" to the latter "vehicle," then bringing the two together. This whole process is a little like stepping through a mirror. The poem begins in the real world, steps through the device of the comparison, which is like a transparent forcefield, and looks back through from the otherworldly side. Then, at the end, the poem starts to step back through the mirror and pauses midway, one leg on one side and one on the other.

Once the viewpoint is over on the otherworldly side, that side (the battery) has begun to feel a little worldly, and the camera has begun to seem a little otherworldly. Thus the poem ends with two real-seeming objects, camera and battery, balanced on either side of the mirror.

I want to repeat, for emphasis, that in composing such a poem, a poet should leave out details from either the worldly or otherworldly sides that cannot be paralleled. I could not have made use of the camera's viewing hole, or rangefinder, because I could not find a parallel in a car battery for this. Nor could I have made use of the battery's two terminal posts, because a box camera has no parallel to this. One parallel I might have made, had I wished to stretch it that far, would have been to show how the battery's carrying-handle was like the handle on top of one of these old box cameras, but not all batteries have these handles, and I felt that it would take up too much of the poem to work in this observation. Besides, to point out that the camera and battery both have handles would be to gain a very minor point, because the reader already knows that both batteries and cameras can be carried about; it is important to give the reader credit for his or her intelligence.

In Jean Cocteau's film about Orpheus, the leading character from time to time passes through a transparent field into another world. To enable himself to do so, he must wear a pair of magic yellow gloves. The yellow gloves for a poet are his or her abilities to draw comparisons or to make associations, and to draw as much power as possible from these.

Now let's examine some more examples of the careful use of figurative language. First I want to look closely at a poem by Linda Pastan.

Pastan's poems are usually quite short. The following one is typical not only of her brevity but also of her fine-tuning of metaphor. I have been talking about the advantages of integrating metaphor, about how to make it part of the integral structure of a poem rather than merely dropping it in as ornament.

◆ NOVEMBER

It is an old drama
this disappearance of the leaves,
this seeming death
of the landscape.
In a later scene,
or earlier,
the trees like gnarled magicians
produce handkerchiefs
of leaves
out of empty branches.

And we watch.
We are like children
at this spectacle
of leaves,
as if one day we too
will open the wooden doors
of our coffins
and come out smiling
and bowing
all over again.

I don't know Linda Pastan, but I strongly suspect that this poem began with a metaphor, that is, leaves appearing at the ends of branches made her think of the handkerchiefs that magicians pull from their sleeves. I say this because this tree/magician metaphor is so deeply integrated in the structure of the poem, holding it together in so many ways, that I doubt if it could be anything other than part of an originating impulse. It would be very difficult to start to write a poem about trees and then to fit such a metaphor over it, like pulling a sock over a foot.

Metaphors are good examples of things being greater than the sum of their parts—two parts to each metaphor: the tenor (in this instance the tree) and the vehicle (the magician). A carefully controlled metaphor, like any clearly observed association of two dissimilar things or events, can excite the responses of readers because it gives them a glimpse of an order that they might not otherwise have become aware of. If you think of a metaphor as being a bridge between two things, it's not the things that are of the most importance, but the grace and lift of the bridge between them, flying high over the surface. To begin writing a poem around a metaphor gets the author a head start toward poetry that has integral order and transcends the mere sum of its accumulated words.

There are many things about magicians that are not like trees, for example, and many things about trees that are not like magicians. Pastan makes no mention of these, but works exclusively with those features that she can relate back and forth. For example, the magicians are described as being gnarled, which is something that we can say about both people and trees. If she had written

> the trees like agile magicians
> produce handkerchiefs

the power of the metaphor would be slightly dissipated because though a magician might be agile, we don't think of trees as being agile, being anchored firmly to the ground as they are. And so on. It will serve you well as a poet to put each of your metaphors to this test: have you used some detail on one side of the bridge that can't be logically mirrored on the other? If you observe that a pile of cannonballs looks like a bunch of grapes, avoid mentioning that cannonballs are very heavy and that grapes are sweet. A metaphor that is not carefully controlled is worse for the prospects of a poem than having no metaphor at all.

Though Pastan abandons the specific leaf/handkerchief metaphor at the end of the fourth line of the second stanza, notice that she now picks up and *follows through* with the magician she has deftly implanted in our imaginations, a magician who, in addition to pulling handkerchiefs out of his sleeves, might miraculously emerge unscathed after being locked in a box. Here she is working for a short time on the vehicle (magician) side of the metaphor, letting herself fly a little, playing with her magician before bringing the poem back to ground with final images that suggest both the leaves and the magician.

My own poem "Etude," from my book *Weather Central*, works in much the same way. Notice the way I drift away into the vehicle side of the metaphorical bridge, the man at his desk, and then bring the poem back to the bird (tenor) at the conclusion:

⇒ ETUDE

> I have been watching a Great Blue Heron
> fish in the cattails, easing ahead
> with the stealth of a lover composing a letter,
> the hungry words looping and blue
> as they coil and uncoil, as they kiss and sting.
>
> Let's say that he holds down an everyday job
> in an office. His blue suit blends in.
> Long days swim beneath the glass top
> of his desk, each one alike. On the lip
> of each morning, a bubble trembles.
>
> No one has seen him there, writing a letter
> to a woman he loves. His pencil is poised
> in the air like the beak of a bird.
> He would spear the whole world if he could,
> toss it and swallow it live.

Here's another example, by Martin Walls:

⇒ SNAIL

> It is a flattened shell the color of spoiled milk, a bold
> Swirl slowly stirred that charts the age of what's
>
> Curled inside with the tension of a watch spring. A creature
> That embodies the history of metaphysics: first it exists,
>
> Then it doesn't, then it emerges once again, unrolls
> One, then another, eyestalk, like periscopes breaking
>
> The surface of its wet-life. And here's the tongue body,
> The petal-body, molding its shape to the world's shape.

Notice the way in which the first metaphor gets followed through. The shell is described as being the color of spoiled milk, a visual characteristic, observed from a distance. And because the author is looking from a distance at the snail's configuration and color, and not tasting the shell or touching it, not putting the snail in his mouth, other characteristics of milk, such as its sweetness, its temperature, are left out of the comparison. But another of the characteristics of milk, its fluidity, can be perceived from a distance, and gets brought in, appropriately, as "swirl slowly stirred."

It would have been a mistake to bring in sensory detail that the viewer wouldn't have experienced, such as:

> It is a flattened shell the color of spoiled milk, a sweet
> Swirl slowly stirred that charts the age of what's . . .

That "sweet" would have spoiled the metaphor.

And while we're talking about observing something from a distance, let's step a little to one side and look at a *prose* passage that I think is useful. The following paragraphs open the first chapter of Douglas C. Jones's *Elkhorn Tavern*, a novel about a minor battle in the Civil War:

> He saw them coming along Wire Road, could almost hear
> the steel-shod hooves on the frozen ground, although they
> were at least a mile away and all he could actually hear
> was the wind in the black locusts around him. They came
> in column, the riders bundled against the late February
> cold under slategray clouds. The breathing of their horses
> created a milky vapor around them, whiter than the few
> remaining drifts of snow lying in shadowed places and
> clinging to the bark on oak and walnut trees.
>
> They had first come into view beyond Elkhorn Tavern,
> bunching and stretching out again on the road through the
> thick timber. It was an undisciplined movement but certain
> in its progress, much as a copperhead snake goes across a
> woodlot in winter, sluggish but deadly. They were armed.
> He could see rifles across saddle horns or thrusting up
> like Indian lances, butts held on thighs. It was a formless
> group, smoke-colored, yet the guns were clear to him, as

were the horses' legs moving and the heads of the riders. He marked the variety of their headgear—wide-brimmed hats and fur caps with flaps hanging out to either side like the helmet horns of raiding Norsemen. Even at a distance, he knew they wore no regular uniforms. He guessed there were about forty of them.

Across the wide, flat valley where dry cornstalks rattled in fields beside woodlots, he watched the leaders turn into the yard of the tavern. Through bare branches of intervening trees, he could see the long-white structure that sat against the wall of limestone high-ground called Pea Ridge.

The riders surrounded the building, engulfing it, some of them running their horses into the rear yard. There was a tiny balloon of smoke from the hand of one who sat his mount before the tavern's front gallery. It took a long time for the report of the shot to reach him, and then the distance and wind turned it soft—the sound of a finger thumped against the side of a hickory barrel.

Beginning writers are often encouraged to use all five of the senses in descriptive writing in order to enhance the reader's identification with the setting. In this excerpt, the primary sense used is sight, and the secondary sense is hearing. Nearly all of what is portrayed is done visually. The observer actually hears only two sounds—the wind in the trees and the muffled shot (he imagines one other sound, that of the rattling cornstalks beyond him). There is no use of taste, touch, or smell.

In the first paragraph, had he wanted to involve more of the senses, Jones had the opportunity to insert a sentence like, "As he stood there with his chin down in his collar, he could smell his breath, sour as vinegar," or he could have written, "His hands were numb even inside his gloves, and the cold penetrated his boots. His toes felt dead as twigs." Why didn't he do something like this? Probably because when we are intensely interested in something we're watching, we aren't as aware of ourselves.

What is the purpose of the phrase "where dry cornstalks rattled in fields beside woodlots"? Since the observer can't possibly hear this distant rattle, why does Jones choose to include it? Though I can only speculate, I think Jones is trying to convey that he has projected himself into the scene in the distance, and is imaginatively creating the sound of the corn.

Notice also how the appropriate choice of figures of speech helps to convey the threat of the advancing company of guerrillas: "much as a copperhead snake goes across a woodlot in winter, sluggish but deadly." The fur caps have earflaps that "resemble the helmet horns of raiding Norsemen."

The effect would have been altogether different, would it not, had Jones described the column as looking like a child's windup toy train, or if the earflaps had looked like the ears of cocker spaniels.

The choice of the elements in a figure of speech always conveys the current mood of the observer. There is little need, in a story or poem, to come right out and tell the reader whether the speaker is happy or sad if you have carefully described the associations he or she is drawing from his or her senses. By writing in this way, the outer world becomes an integral part of the effect, subtly shaded by emotion, rather than merely providing a fixed backdrop before which the action takes place.

I've talked a lot about the importance of having the various elements in a metaphor work together, but all rules are meant to be broken, and the first stanza of this poem by Maurya Simon takes a chance on being inconsistent, and does it, I think, to very good effect.

➠ BLUE MOVIES

> His fingers are caterpillars balanced
> on the bough of her body.
> Her legs snake around his trunk,
> her arms entwine over his broad back.
>
> The moans of the lovers float
> above the heads of the Latino ushers,
> past the ticket office where ID is required,
> to the old men who are waiting in line
> outside the theater in the black drizzle.
> Some hold umbrellas as if they were candles,

others collect their breath in their hands.
One man studies a small red mole
protruding from the ticket taker's lip.

The line moves forward.
Thank you, they say, as they move out
of one darkness into another.

The metaphor of the first two lines sets up the woman as a tree and the man's fingers as caterpillars, then the third and fourth lines confuse this by changing the man into a tree about which the woman snakes. The woman is both tree and snake, the man is both caterpillar and tree. This results in some confusion of images in the reader's mind, the woman and man shifting between forms. Why this works well in this particular poem may be that both metaphors, disparate but working together, convey the confusion of the lovemaking scene on the movie screen, as well as its exotic strangeness to the people in the audience.

The last lines of the poem are masterful in their use of double entendre. There is the literal darknesses of the rainy street and the movie house (note that the umbrellas are like candles!), and the figurative darknesses, both of the men's loneliness as they wait in line and of the pornography within the theater.

Poetry has enriched my life in many ways, but perhaps most by helping me see what I call the Marvelous Connections. Uh-oh, you may be thinking, here comes the Spiritual Life stuff! But please, indulge me a little.

Growing older cured the acne of my adolescent atheism, thinned the hair of my middle-aged skepticism, and left me as a doddering geezer with a firm belief that there is indeed a mysterious order to the universe. If I should live another twenty years, I may one day discover I believe in a god who holds a keen interest in Ted Kooser's personal welfare, though it seems pretty unlikely. But, specific to this chapter, I do believe in a universal order and, when it comes to poetry, the best poems seem to reach through the opaque surface of the world and give us a glimpse of an order beyond.

If I understand what he wrote, Ralph Waldo Emerson suggested that there might be a plane of common unity among all things and occurrences that he called the Oversoul, and that all things touch each other on and along that plane. Emerson was a poet and not a physicist. Many years later, the physicist-proponents of the big bang theory suggested that all things in the universe have spread forward in time from one highly compressed speck of matter. According to the big bang, all things are related, made up of the same elements and energies and governed by the same laws. For me, this bears out Emerson, and I like it immensely that a poet had the idea first. Poets may go at the big truths a little cattywampus, but sometimes they do get to them.

The second section of the following poem by Mekeel McBride seems to be suggesting what I've been talking about:

⇒ A BLESSING

> Freely chosen, discipline
> is absolute freedom.—Ron Serino

I.

The blue shadow of dawn settles
its awkward silks into the enamelled kitchen
and soon you will wake with me into the long
discipline of night and day—the morning sky
startled and starred with returning birds.
You half-whisper, half sigh, "This will never stop."
And I say, "Look at the constellations
our keys and coins make, there,
on the polished sky of the dresser top."

II.

From what sometimes seems an arbitrary
form of discipline often come two words
that rhyme and in the rhyming fully marry
the world of spoons and sheets and common birds
to another world that we have always known
where the waterfall of dawn does not drown
even the haloed gnat; where we are shown
how to find and hold the pale day moon, round
and blessed in the silver lake of a coffee spoon.

By "two words / that rhyme and in the rhyming fully marry / the world of spoons and sheets and common birds / to another world that we have always known," I think McBride can be seen to be talking about the transformation brought about, through poetry, of one order into another, higher order.

In Robert Bly's translation of Tomas Tranströmer's poem, "The Couple," a marvelous thing happens in the first sentence:

> They turn the light off, and its white globe glows
> an instant and then dissolves, like a tablet
> in a glass of darkness.

Though I've read this poem dozens of times, this figure of speech, in this instance a simile, has never lost its power over me. Here a simile is a more effective choice than a metaphor would have been. Can you feel the subtle difference? If a metaphor had been used . . .

> They turn the light off, and its white globe glows
> an instant and then dissolves, a tablet
> in a glass of darkness

the speaker would have been a little too sure of his observations. The simile adds some human vulnerability.

The power of a figure of speech seems to grow as the distance increases between the readers' personal associations with the things compared. Robert Bly has written about this, describing metaphor as "leaping" from one part of the brain to another. To say that a green delicious apple is like a Granny Smith apple is not likely to get anybody's attention, or to produce any kind of a feeling of revelation, but to suggest that a fading light bulb is like a dissolving tablet is more of a leap—almost, I think, an epiphany.

But besides showing us this marvelous connection between the light bulb and the tablet, something else is going on: Tranströmer (or Bly, working with Tranströmer's Swedish) carefully controls his metaphor so as not to admit any associations that might diminish the effect. Just as in the examples given earlier in this chapter, Tranströmer/Bly does this by *selecting out* any aspects of tablets and light bulbs that have nothing in common. For example, he doesn't write

> They turn the light off, and its hot globe glows
> an instant and then dissolves, like a tablet
> in a glass of darkness

because, though a light bulb is hot, a tablet in water is cool. He doesn't write

> They turn the light off, and its white globe glows
> an instant and then dissolves, like a tablet hissing
> in a glass of darkness

because though a tablet might hiss, a light bulb doesn't. Notice also that he doesn't write

> They turn the light off, and its white globe glows
> an instant and then dissolves, like a tablet
> in a glass of water

because, even though it could be seen to be an accurate description, he is not writing about water but about light and darkness, and there is a cleaner, brighter spark of sudden revelation with *darkness*.

When you are working with your own poems, keep in mind that the power of a metaphor may come not only in proportion to the distance between its elements, but also through the author's use of controls, so that the dazzling spark that suddenly arcs from one side of the comparison to the other is a clean flash, not dimmed by extraneous matter floating between. The poet's goal is to light up the sky. The poet, Tranströmer/Bly, would have much weakened the spark if he had written

> They turn the light off, and its hot globe glows
> an instant and then dissolves, like a tablet hissing
> in a glass of water.

Yet this is the way lots of poets write, and it is one reason their metaphors may not be quite as good a glimpse into the universal order as this one is.

I'd like to conclude this chapter with an example of a poem that uses no metaphor at all, just to show you that metaphor and similes aren't always necessary in constructing a successful poem. It's by Susan Mitchell.

→ THE DEATH

I heard the crying and came closer.
Father was sitting in the half-filled bathtub.
He wasn't covering his face with his hands.
He was crying into the air.
Mother was washing him. She ran the soapy cloth
round and round on his chest.
After a while, he sat on the side of the tub
and she dried him.
Then he took the towel and put it over his face.

I walked out of the house certain I would not come back.
Downstairs a neighbor's daughter was tearing
leaves off a hedge. When we rubbed the leaves into our hands
our hands turned green. I put my green hands
on her face and wondered where I would go
now that I was never coming back.
I walked to the subway station
and for hours I watched the trains going east
to Coney Island. Then I went back.

When Mother told me
we were sitting in the car, just the two of us.
I must have climbed
out of the front seat because
I see myself sitting alone in the back
in the not quite dark. I have taken
my father's canvas hat from the floor
and put it on my head. Through its visor
the first green night is coming on.
A green woman is rocking a green carriage.
A green man sits and smokes on his green stoop.

Sometimes, when the narrative of an experience is strong enough, and unique enough, it doesn't require much more than a carefully written, straight-ahead, unadorned delivery. If somebody is reporting a fatal car accident, it may not be in the poem's interest to describe the smashed-up vehicles as looking like tea roses with their petals falling away. Metaphor can seem condescending or inappropriate in situations like that. It's inappropriate to take as your subject somebody's misfortune and make of it a literary event.

There are several things in "The Death" toward which I'd like to direct your attention.

First, notice how clipped and declarative is the language, much like that which we could expect from a person telling a painful story, biting off the ends of the sentences, using full stops in order to take a little sip of breath and regather his or her composure.

Second, notice that the principal details are unique and unpredictable, not the sorts of things we'd expect somebody to make up, details that enhance the poem's authenticity. We feel that the poet, speaking as a child, had to actually have been there, on the spot, to have seen these unusual, unexpected things: the father grieving in the bathtub, the neighbor girl tearing leaves off the hedge, the canvas hat with the green plastic visor. The spare, declarative language gives the poem a great deal of force.

This chapter is not meant to suggest that the primary items on the "parts list" for poetry include only metaphors, similes, and careful description. For example, though Mitchell doesn't use simile and metaphor, notice her use of repetition—"When we rubbed the leaves into our hands / our hands turned green. I put my green hands / on her face"—as well as her use of understatement throughout. All these are tools as well.

CHAPTER TWELVE

Relax and Wait

Time and patience turn the mulberry leaf to silk.
—Serbian proverb

You've written your poem. The first step in spotting its flaws is a simple one. Set aside what you've written and let it cool off for a while, the longer the better. Take a look at it after twenty-four hours if you must, tinker with it a little. Does there seem to be an awkward rhythm in one of the lines? Are there places that could use more specific detail? And so on. Then set it aside again for as long as you can stand to. Like a petri dish, the longer you leave a poem by itself the more stinky fungus will surface. As Edward Weeks said, "When the ideas begin to run smoothly they can so easily run away with us, leaving behind pages which in a colder mood seem full of extravagance." Extravagance, certainly, but just plain stupidity, too.

If you can manage to do it, leave your poem alone till it begins to look as if somebody else might have written it. Then you can see it for what it is, a creation independent of you, out on its own. A poem must be equipped to thrive by itself in a largely indifferent world. You can't be there with it, like its parent, offering explanations, saying to a confused reader, "Yes, but here's what I *meant!*" A poem has to do all of its own explaining.

What's the hurry? The truth is, *nobody's waiting for you to press your poetry into their hands.* Nobody knows you're writing it, nobody's hungry for it, nobody's dying to get at it. Not a living soul has big expectations for the success of your poem other than you. Of course, *you want it* to be wonderful—pure genius, beautiful, heartbreaking, memorable—and by coincidence that's just the kind of writing your audience would like to be reading. So let time show you some of the things you've done wrong before you show your poem to somebody and are embarrassed by a problem, or two or three problems, that you just couldn't see in the exhilaration of just having written it.

And don't stop writing while you're waiting for one poem to mature. Most of us are tempted to wait for approval before moving on. We want our mothers to praise our mud pies before we make any more. But if you're going to get better at writing, you have to write a lot. You have to press on. Isak Dinesen said, "Write a little every day, without hope, without despair." When you finish a draft, or get stuck, put it out of your sight in a drawer. After a month or so, you can take out that poem and the others with it and start looking through them, beginning with the oldest. You'll be amazed at the way in which the passage of time has helped you come up with solutions to problems you had during those early drafts. You'll also be surprised at how awkward some of it may seem.

Don't worry that the process of revision seems slow. The writer's tools were developed early—paper, pen, and ink; a watchful eye; an open heart—and good writing is still the patient handiwork of those simple tools. A poet who makes only one really fine poem during his life gives far more to the world than the poet who publishes twenty books of mediocre verse. The Industrial Revolution did not reach imaginative writing until recently, and today black clouds of soot belch from the smokestacks over the creative writing schools. Poems get manufactured and piled on the loading docks where many of them rot for lack of transport. Wouldn't we all be better off if there wasn't such an emphasis on productivity?

At a party, I once heard a woman say that it was "criminal" that Harper Lee had written only the one novel, *To Kill a Mockingbird*. What peculiar expectations we've developed for our writers! "Criminal?" We ought to be thankful Lee used her time to write her book as perfectly as she could, that she didn't rush a lot of half-finished books into print.

So just relax. There's plenty of time to do your writing well and, if you're lucky, to make a poem or two that might make a difference.

LEARNING FROM PROSE

Here's something else you might try while you're waiting for your poem to age. Because readers are so much more at ease with prose, redrafting your poem as prose can sometimes be helpful. Without destroying your original version, write out another as prose, running from margin to margin. Don't change anything, just drop the line endings. You may be surprised at how clumsy your words may look when you see them as prose. Do some of your sentences look like they're standing on their heads? Are there any of those awkwardnesses like "Throw Mama from the train a kiss?"

Some poets even start with prose. I know a teacher who asks his poetry writing students to compose essays and then transform them into poems. He finds that for beginning writers this makes the process of writing a poem less intimidating. The student moves forward from prose, with which he or she is more comfortable, into the poem, which is new and discomfiting territory. Although I haven't studied this teacher's results, it's my guess that the poems that arise out of this process are more clear and accessible than the poems composed without this step. This technique takes into consideration that poetry writing is a process, the development of an impulse into a finished work.

Of course, there are disadvantages of moving from poetry to prose and back again. We know that we can't come up with a poem simply by cutting prose into lengths and scattering it in lines down the page. It won't feel like poetry. It will feel a little too loose, too watered down. The energies of prose are generally less tightly controlled than those of poetry. Poems employ various devices like line endings and rhythm to heighten their effects. Sometimes a poem seems to heat up with energy just because it has been restrained by its form. A horse may be beautiful running at top speed, but a horse appears to be even more powerful when it has been reined in and is wild-eyed and snorting and pawing the air with its hooves.

ASKING FOR HELP

We write, we read what we've written, then we rewrite again and again. It's just us with our poem, hour after hour, like Jacob wrestling with the angel. Eventually we think we've done everything in our power to make that poem as good as we could. We want to show what we've written to somebody. It's natural to want to know how well we've communicated. So go ahead, if you have somebody to ask, ask. As my friend and fellow writer Steve Cox says, writing can be like folding bedsheets or banquet-sized tablecloths; you can do it yourself, but it can be a little easier if you can find somebody to help. The acknowledgments page of just about any book (including this one!) will show you how much authors have depended upon assistance and how grateful they are for receiving it.

As a beginning writer, your biggest need for help is likely to be in making your writing understandable and interesting, and there may be no way to tell how you're doing without asking somebody to read what you've written. For one thing, it's very difficult for most of us to identify our own grammatical errors. That's because each if us writes at the top of our knowledge of grammar and we aren't smart enough to see our own mistakes. This helper doesn't have to be a writer, but he or she does have to be somebody you can trust to be honest.

What you want from this first helper is relatively uncomplicated. You want to know whether your writing makes sense and whether it is engaging. Anybody who likes to read will suffice, if he or she can be trusted to tell you the truth and is willing to put in the time and energy to read what you have written and then to talk with you about it. You might ask your spouse or partner, a neighbor, or a good-humored friend to be your first reader—someone who is willing to help you get a sense of how well your writing succeeds in reaching across the gulf between writer and reader.

Ask one or two people to read your poem aloud to you. Don't let them rehearse. Ask them to read it aloud without looking at it first. Listen carefully for where they stumble and get hung up, for places where they trip over the vocabulary or the rhythm. Samuel Taylor Coleridge said poetry is the best words in the best order. That's part of what you're listening for. You can learn an enormous amount about your poem through this simple process. And after this sometimes unsettling experience you may have enough revisions to make to keep you at your desk awhile longer.

It may be best if the first person you ask to look at your work doesn't have an English professor's arsenal of critical terms. The slightest intimation of disapproval from a "professional" can be so discouraging and intimidating that it can stop you dead in your tracks just at the time when you need to write and write and write to get better at it.

There are many examples of writers who have maintained lifelong associations with other writers to their mutual benefit. Leonard Nathan, who is mentioned elsewhere in this book, was a stranger to me when I wrote him a postcard to tell him I admired a poem he had published in a magazine. We struck up a correspondence that eventually became a regular exchange that has flourished for over thirty years.

One temptation to be avoided when asking for help is to inquire, "Is this any good?" The last thing you need is a value judgment, and you can never be sure that any reader will answer that one candidly. It's the writer's equivalent of "Does this dress make me look fat?" or "Isn't my new granddaughter a pretty baby?" Instead, you need to ask your first reader some value-neutral questions like "Does this seem clear to you?" and "Can you think of ways I could make this more interesting?"

You need a reader who will be candid, who will take the time to talk about specifics. It won't do you any good to have someone who simply says, "Well, it's really *different!*" You want somebody who will say, "In the third line of the second stanza, well, I may be really dumb, but I don't know what you mean by the word 'belletristic.'" When you have a helper who isn't afraid to ask dumb questions—that's a reader worth listening to.

Specific comments are far more useful than general ones, though if somebody tells you they "really like" your writing, you might as well enjoy the comment before you ask the tough question, "Well, what was it *exactly* that you liked? And was there anything you *didn't* like, maybe just a little?"

Two beginning writers, neither of whom knows a whole lot about writing, can teach one another to appreciate the value of specific comments. Though it's nice to receive praise such as, "I really like this!" what you both really need is, "I don't understand how the umbrella stand in this poem got over under the parlor window when a couple of stanzas back it was just inside the kitchen door." Specific comments like that can be invaluable.

One way to elicit specific comments is to ask your helper to read the poem when convenient and to write notes for you to study later.

Reading and criticizing somebody's writing requires concentration, and your helper will probably appreciate not being put on the spot by being asked to respond immediately. It can be uncomfortable to have a manuscript pushed under your nose with the expectation that you'll read it immediately and say what you think. Just as you might appreciate time to form your remarks, so will your helper. You two may find you get the most out of your writing friendship when you correspond by letters or e-mail. In that way, you can study and restudy your helper's comments.

When you've been assured that your helper is willing to be candid, and when your helper sees that you are willing and eager to rewrite in the light of his or her comments, you'll both gain confidence in your working relationship. Then you can ask more pointed questions: "Are there places where your mind drifted away?" and "What would you omit?" and "What more would you like to know?"

People have begun to use the Internet to set up writers' groups, and that may be a good answer for you if you can't find people in your community with an interest in writing. The problem with Internet discussion groups is that you are alone among strangers, some of them kooks, whereas in a writers' group you have a better sense of who is trying to help you.

WRITING GROUPS

You might consider starting a writing group or joining one that is already meeting. No matter how small the community, you are likely to find a few people who like to write, are hungry for encouragement, and want to get better at it. And four or five people are all you need. Churches, community rec centers, YWCAs, YMCAs, clubs, community college courses, professional associations, and informal groups are good places to start. You may have met others who are writing, and you can suggest getting together once a month or every couple of weeks to talk about your efforts.

Some groups have a revolving schedule under which a quarter of the members are due to hand out something one week and the next quarter the next week and so on. In that way there is work to discuss at each meeting, work that has been carefully studied by all the members on their own schedules. You don't want the group to get too big because each weekly meeting won't afford enough time to cover all the comments. Twelve people is a good maximum, with three of the members up for criticism each week.

When you show up for your first meeting, take a deep breath before you ring the doorbell and get yourself ready for constructive criticism and not for praise. Of course you want praise. The desire for praise and adulation, even love, is one of a writer's chief drives. And if it comes, enjoy it. But if somebody says, "I think this poem is really wonderful," it's fair play to ask, "Could you tell me what about it you find wonderful?" When somebody says you've done something well, you need to know specifically what that something is, so you can do it again.

Ideally, the members of the group all encourage each other and give each other very careful and thoughtful practical criticism. With luck, the members of the group build a strong bond of friendship and do not compete with each other as writers. They agree to:

1. Encourage each other.
2. Make specific constructive criticism—not "I really like this" or "I don't much care for that" but "Your first stanza seems like you're just warming up to write the next stanza. Perhaps you should consider starting with the second stanza." Specific criticism is useful, general comments are not.
3. Not take themselves too seriously. Have fun.
4. Avoid using "bad" and "good." Bad and good are useful in describing human behavior, because nearly all of us agree that a person's actions can be seen to arise out of goodness or badness, but these two words are not at all helpful when describing literary works. They ought to be banned from the discussion of writing. A person can be bad or good, but generally, a poem or story cannot. Yet we often hear people saying, "That's a bad poem" or "I just read a really good poem." When we hear people say that a poem is bad, what they are really saying is that, for personal reasons, they don't like it. They may not like the manner in which it is written, they may not like the

effect it has on them, and so on. When they say it is good they are saying they like it. We have individual likes and dislikes about practically everything. I dislike broccoli because I don't like the way it feels in my mouth, like chewing pieces of sponge, but broccoli isn't *bad*.

SUBMITTING POEMS FOR PUBLICATION

OK. You can't wait any longer. You're looking for approval for what you've written, and you want to see if someone will publish your poetry. Grit your teeth and be prepared for rejection. It's my estimation that less than 1 percent of poems submitted to magazines get published, and many of those after repeated rejection. I suppose that in my forty-odd years of sending work out I have received more than a thousand rejection slips, but perseverance pays, and I have also published several hundred poems. Here are some thoughts about submission for publication.

FINDING PLACES TO SUBMIT

The *International Directory of Little Magazines and Small Presses* costs around $35, but it is by far the very best investment you can make when looking for places to submit. It is published by Dustbooks, PO Box 100, Paradise CA 95967. The Web site is www.dustbooks.com. It's an annual publication, but I've found that if I buy a copy every few years I'm kept pretty well up to date on what's out there. Right now I'm using an issue that's three years old. After all, magazines of quality are the ones you want to publish in, and they're the ones that have endured for at least a few years.

One advantage of the *International Directory* is that since it is not a place where national periodicals list their current needs and wants, the journals listed receive a smaller number of submissions.

Newsstand magazines for writers list places that are open to unsolicited manuscripts, but tens of thousands of people read these popular listings. When a magazine looking for poems lists its name there it's likely to be inundated with submissions. The more submissions a journal receives, the less chance your work will be able to catch an editor's attention. You're likely to have better luck by going to your library and reading through literary magazines and submitting to those you like. I said earlier that we write the kinds of poems we like to read, and if you can find a journal publishing poems you like, there's a chance you're writing poems that might be welcome there.

When the word gets around creative writing circles that someone has gotten a poem accepted in some journal, then everybody decides they too ought to submit there. Most journals would like to appear to be eclectic, and none is going to want to publish a whole group of poets from a writing group in Boise, Idaho, no matter how good the poetry is.

It isn't at all smart to submit to a literary magazine unless you've either looked at a sample copy or had somebody recommend it. There is nothing quite so embarrassing as to have a poem accepted and then, when you receive your complimentary copies, to find that the contents are disappointing if not just awful. I was thrilled as a very young man to have an early poem accepted in an anthology I had never seen that I saw advertised in a newspaper, and then I got a letter saying that if I wanted a copy of the issue with my poem I could buy one from them for something like $12, which was a lot more in 1960 than it is today. The editors must have accepted every poem they received, because there were hundreds included, one by each poet. Cheaply printed and bound, too. I'd guess that most of those fledgling poets, like me, bought copies. Somebody made a whole lot of money off the vanity of the rest of us. Live and learn. People are still putting out anthologies like that today. If you see an ad in a newspaper announcing a contest and calling for poems, chances are it's a venture like the one I'm describing.

GETTING YOUR SUBMISSION READY TO GO

Always send fresh copies of poems, not ones that have been folded again and again or have coffee stains or paper clip marks. You might even use really nice paper, like cotton rag resume stock. You want your submission to look as if you care about it.

Don't forget to enclose a stamped, self-addressed envelope with enough postage.

Three to five poems is about right for most magazines, but check your sample copy for instructions about submission.

Put your name, mailing address, phone numbers and e-mail addresses, single spaced, in either the upper left-hand or right-hand corner of each poem. I don't recommend using a professional mailing address or an academic title. That can look pretentious. Most editors don't care that you are an assistant professor and some will think you have an inflated sense of yourself if you say so.

If your poem is more than one page in length, the second and subsequent pages can include your name, the title, and page number, as in: Wordsworth, "Preludes," p. 2. Don't staple or paper clip the pages.

Poems can be single-spaced or double-spaced, but I usually use one and a half spaces, which to me looks more readable. If by using single-space you can get a longer poem onto one page, do that.

If you can't come up with five really strong poems, send four. Don't send four good ones and one weak one. One rotten apple spoils the whole barrel. I have from time to time submitted just one or two poems if I thought they might be just what that magazine might like.

I've edited literary magazines and have a deep prejudice against multiple submissions, that is, submitting the same poem to more than one magazine simultaneously. Unless I get the feeling that the poet is interested in appearing in my magazine, I'm not going to be very interested in his or her work. Multiple submissions have the look of desperation. And if by some chance your poem gets accepted by two journals, you'll have to write to one of them to apologize and you'll probably never get an acceptance there again. However, some journals advertise that multiple submissions are acceptable. God knows why they want to subject themselves to that, but that's their choice.

Never burn a bridge. Be grateful. Send thanks. If a magazine accepts your work it is a good sign it may take other of your poems. Over a period of years you can establish good relationships with particular journals, and they can be counted on to pay special attention to your submissions.

Cover letters are OK, so long as they don't brag too much about how important you are, having had recent work in *Sweep Up the Bitter Dregs Review* and *Absolutely the Last Ditch Quarterly*. If, however, you have work forthcoming in highly respected journals like the *Kenyon Review* or *Ploughshares*, you might mention that. Be brief and to the point. Editors have very little patience for wordy cover letters.

After your poems have been rejected several times, it may be foolhardy to keep sending them out. If three or four respectable journals have turned them down, chances are the poems have something seriously wrong with them and should be set aside for further revision. If you send a poem to fifty journals and one finally takes it, you can be assured that that journal is not in the first rank—or the second or even the third rank—of literary magazines, and when you get your complimentary copy you may be mortified by the company you're keeping.

I wish you good luck with your writing, friend, and I hope that you'll write a few poems that someone will want to show to the world by publishing them. Remember that the greatest pleasures of writing are to be found in the process itself. Enjoy paying attention to the world, relish the quiet hours at your desk, delight in the headiness of writing well and the pleasure of having done something as well as you can.

Here's one last poem, a favorite of mine, by one of our country's most inventive and accessible poets, Nancy Willard. Earlier in this book I talked about how poems can give us new ways of looking at the world. This is just such a poem.

→ NIGHT LIGHT

The moon is not green cheese.
It is china and stands in this room.
It has a ten-watt bulb and a motto:
Made in Japan.

Whey-faced, doll-faced,
it's closed as a tooth
and cold as the dead are cold
till I touch the switch.

Then the moon performs
its one trick:
it turns into a banana.
It warms to its subjects,

it draws us into its light,
just as I knew it would
when I gave ten dollars
to the pale clerk

in the store that sold
everything.
She asked, did I have a car?
She shrouded the moon in tissue

and laid it to rest in a box.
The box did not say Moon.
It said This side up.
I tucked the moon into my basket

and bicycled into the world.
By the light of the sun
I could not see the moon
under my sack of apples,

moon under slab of salmon,
moon under clean laundry,
under milk its sister
and bread its brother,

moon under meat.
Now supper is eaten.
Now laundry is folded away.
I shake out the old comforters.

My nine cats find their places
and go on dreaming where they left off.
My son snuggles under the heap.
His father loses his way in a book.

It is time to turn on the moon.
It is time to live by a different light.

REFERENCES AND SOURCE ACKNOWLEDGMENTS

Following each reference is the chapter of this book in which the quotation appears.

Addonizio, Kim. "Aquarium." In *The Philosopher's Club*. Brockport NY: BOA Editions, Ltd., 1994. [chapter 4]

Akmahtova, Anna. "We walk along the hard crest of the snowdrift," translated from the Russian by Jane Kenyon. English translation copyright 1999 by the Estate of Jane Kenyon. Reprinted from *A Hundred White Daffodils* with the permission of Graywolf Press, St. Paul MN. [chapter 9]

Amichai, Yehuda. "I Walked Past a House Where I Lived Once." In *The Selected Poetry of Yehuda Amichai*. Berkeley: University of California Press, 1966. [chapter 8]

Ammons, A. R. "Winter Scene." In *Collected Poems, 1951–1971*. New York: W. W. Norton, 1972. Used by permission of W. W. Norton & Co., Inc. [chapter 1]

Baxter, Charles. *Saul and Patsy*. New York: Pantheon Books, 2003. [chapter 9]

Berger, John. *Selected Essays*. New York: Vintage Books, 2001. [chapter 4]

Birkerts, Sven. *Gettysburg Review* 10, no. 2 (Summer 1997): 248. [chapter 2]

Bly, Robert. "Looking at a Dead Wren in My Hand." In *Eating the Honey of Words: New and Selected Poems*. New York: HarperCollins, 1999. Used by permission of Robert Bly. [chapter 5]

———. "The Dead Seal near McClure's Beach." In *Eating the Honey of Words: New and Selected Poems*. New York: HarperCollins, 1999. Used by permission of Robert Bly. [chapter 9]

Burnard, Bonnie. *The Good House*. New York: Henry Holt, 1999. [chapter 8]

Burr, Gray. "A Skater's Waltz." In *A Controversy of Poets*. Garden City NY: Anchor Books, 1965. [chapter 11]

Carter, Jared. "At the Sign-Painter's." In *Work, for the Night is Coming*. New York: Macmillan Publishing Co., Inc., 1981. First published in *Backcountry*. Copyright (c) 1980, 1981, 1995 by Jared Carter and reproduced by permission. [chapter 9]

————. "Fire Burning in a Fifty-Five Gallon Drum." From *Situation Normal.* First published in *The Reaper.* Copyright (c) 1981, 1991 by Jared Carter and reproduced by permission. [chapter 1]

Costanzo, Gerald. "Washington Park" first appeared in *Prairie Schooner* and is reprinted from *Nobody Lives on Arthur Godfrey Boulevard* by Gerald Costanzo. Rochester NY: BOA Editions, Ltd., 1992. [chapter 9]

de la Mare, Walter. "The Listeners." In *The Listeners and Other Poems.* London: Constable & Company, 1912. [chapter 1]

Dickinson, Emily. "It's all I have to bring today." In *The Complete Poems of Emily Dickinson.* Boston: Little, Brown & Co., 1960. [chapter 3]

Evans, David Allan. "Neighbors." In *Train Windows.* Athens: Ohio University Press, 1976. Originally published in *Shenandoah* (Summer 1971). [chapter 9]

————. "The Story of Lava." In *Train Windows.* Athens: Ohio University Press, 1976. First appeared in *Poetry Now.* [chapter 10]

Fairchild, B. H. "There is Constant Movement in My Head." In *The System of Which the Body is One Part.* Brockport NY: State Street Press, 1988. [chapter 5]

Finkle, Donald. "Sonic Boom." In *Selected Shorter Poems.* New York: Atheneum, 1987. [chapter 9]

Fowles, John. Review of *The News from Ireland* by William Trevor. *Atlantic Monthly,* August 1986. [chapter 2]

Francis, Robert. "Glass." In *Collected Poems: 1936–1976.* Amherst: University of Massachusetts Press, 1976. [chapter 7]

————. "Sheep." In *Collected Poems: 1936–1976.* Copyright (c) 1976 by Robert Francis and published by the University of Massachusetts Press, Amherst. [chapter 10]

Genoways, Ted. "Night Train." In *Bullroarer: A Sequence.* Boston: Northeastern University Press, 2001. [chapter 10]

Ghiselin, Brewster. "Rattlesnake." In *Windrose: Poems, 1929–1979.* Salt Lake City: University of Utah Press, 1980. Published by permission of the University of Utah Press and Michael Ghiselin. [chapter 3]

Greene, Jonathan. "Vestige." In *Inventions of Necessity: Selected Poems.* Frankfort KY: Gnomon Press, 1998. Used by permission of Gnomon Press. [chapter 10]

Guest, Edgar. "Mother." In *A Heap o' Livin'.* Chicago: Reilly & Lee Co., 1919. [chapter 6]

Hirshfield, Jane. "Language Wakes Up in the Morning: A Meander toward Writing." *Alaska Quarterly Review* 21, nos. 1 and 2 (2003): 9–22. [chapter 1]

————. "The Envoy." In *Given Sugar, Given Salt*. Copyright (c) 2001 by Jane Hir-
shfield. Reprinted by permission of HarperCollins Publishers, Inc. [chapter
8]

Hopkins, Gerard Manley. "The Windhover." In *Poems and Prose of Gerard Manley
Hopkins*. Harmondsworth, Middlesex UK: Penguin Books, 1953. [chapter 7]

Hugo, Richard. "Letter to Kathy From Wisdom." In *31 Letters and 13 Dreams*.
New York: W. W. Norton & Co., Inc., 1977. [chapter 6]

————. *The Triggering Town*. New York: W. W. Norton & Co., Inc., 1979.
[chapter 1]

Hutchison, Joseph. "Artichoke." In *The Undersides of Leaves*. Denver: Wayland
Press, 1985. [chapter 1]

Hyde, Louis. *The Gift: Imagination and the Erotic Life of Property*. New York: Vintage
Books, 1983. [introduction]

Jones, Douglas. *Elkhorn Tavern*. New York: Holt, Rinehart & Winston, 1980.
[chapter 11]

Kenyon, Jane. "In the Nursing Home," copyright 1996 by the estate of Jane
Kenyon. Reprinted from *Otherwise: New and Selected Poems* with the permission
of Graywolf Press, St. Paul MN. [chapter 6]

Kooser, Ted. "Abandoned Farmhouse." In *Sure Signs*. Pittsburgh: University of
Pittsburgh Press, 1980. [chapter 1]

————. "After Years." In *Delights & Shadows*. Port Townsend WA: Copper
Canyon Press, 2004. [chapter 6]

————. "Camera." In *One World at a Time*. Pittsburgh: University of Pittsburgh
Press, 1985. [chapter 11]

————. "Cosmetics Department." In *Delights & Shadows*. Port Townsend WA:
Copper Canyon Press, 2004. [chapter 9]

————. "Etude." In *Weather Central*. Pittsburgh: University of Pittsburgh Press,
1994. [chapter 11]

————. "A Poetry Reading." In *Weather Central*. Pittsburgh: University of
Pittsburgh Press, 1994. [chapter 1]

————. "A Rainy Morning." In *Delights & Shadows*. Port Townsend WA: Copper
Canyon Press, 2004. [chapter 1]

————. "Student." In *Delights & Shadows*. Port Townsend WA: Copper Canyon
Press, 2004. [chapter 11]

————. "The Possible Lives." *Hudson Review* 56, no. 4 (Winter 2004): 628.
[chapter 11]

————. "Weather Sestina." *Luna*, no. 6 (2003). [chapter 5]

Kuticka, Thea S. "Newcastle Bar & Grill." In *Working Hard for the Money: America's Working Poor in Stories, Poems, and Photos*. Huron OH: Bottom Dog Press, 2002. [chapter 9]

Lux, Thomas. "Shaving the Graveyard." In *New and Selected Poems: 1975–1995*. Boston: Houghton Mifflin Co., 1997. [chapter 8]

McBride, Mekeel. "A Blessing" is reprinted from *The Going Under of the Evening Land* by Carnegie Mellon University Press, Pittsburgh. (c) 1983 by permission of Mekeel McBride. [chapter 11]

Mitchell, Susan. "The Death." In *The Water Inside the Water*. New York: Harper-Collins, 1994. [chapter 11]

Morgan, Robert. "Bellrope." In *At the Edge of Orchard Country*. Middletown CT: Wesleyan University Press, 1987. [chapter 3]

Nevelson, Louise. *Dawns and Dusks*. New York: Charles Scribner's Sons, 1976. [chapter 1]

Niedecker, Lorine. "Popcorn-Can Cover." In *Lorine Niedecker: Collected Works*. Berkeley: University of California Press, 2002. [chapter 10]

Nurkse, D. "Searchers." In *Burnt Island*. New York: Alfred A. Knopf, 2004. Reprinted by permission of Dennis Nurkse and Alfred A. Knopf. [chapter 9]

Oliver, Mary. "Breakage." In *Why I Wake Early*. Copyright (c) 2004 by Mary Oliver. First published in *Poetry*. Reprinted by permission of Beacon Press, Boston. [chapter 11]

Partridge, Dixie Lee. "Fish." In *Watermark*. Montclair NJ: Saturday Press, Inc., 1991. [chapter 6]

Pastan, Linda. "November." In *Carnival Evening: New and Selected Poems, 1968–1998*. Copyright (c) 1998 by Linda Pastan. Used by permission of W. W. Norton & Co., Inc. [chapter 11]

Rash, Ron. "The Men Who Raised the Dead." *Sewanee Review* 109, no. 4 (Fall 2001). [chapter 4]

Ray, David. "At the Train Station in Pamplona." In *The Touched Life: Poets Now 4*. Metuchen NJ: Scarecrow Press, 1982. [chapter 9]

Shapiro, Karl. "Mongolian Idiot." In *Collected Poems: 1940–1978*. New York: Random House, 1978. [chapter 4]

Simon, Maurya. "Blue Movies." *The Enchanted Room*. Port Townsend WA: Copper Canyon Press, 1986. [chapter 11]

Smith, R. T. "Hardware Sparrows." In *Messenger*. Baton Rouge: Louisiana State University Press, 2001. [chapter 3]

Steele, Frank. "Parents." *Blue Sofa Review* 2, no. 1 (Spring 2000): 20. [chapter 8]

Stroud, Joseph. "And I Raised My Hand in Return." In *Below Cold Mountain*. Port Townsend WA: Copper Canyon Press, 1988. [chapter 3]

Su Tung-p'o. *Selected Poems of Su Tung-p'o*, translated by Burton Watson. Port Townsend WA: Copper Canyon Press, 1994. [chapter 4]

Swenson, May. "The Even Sea." In *Nature: Poems Old and New*. Boston: Houghton Mifflin Co., 1994. [chapter 11]

Taylor, Henry. "The Hayfork." *Shenandoah/Strongly Spent* 53, nos. 1–2 (2003): 214. Reprinted from *Shenandoah: The Washington and Lee University Review* with the permission of the editor and the author. [chapter 8]

Tranströmer, Tomas. "Morning Bird Songs." In *The Half-Finished Heaven: The Best Poems of Tomas Tranströmer*, translated by Robert Bly. St. Paul MN: Graywolf Press, 2001. [chapter 1]

————. "The Couple." In *The Half-Finished Heaven: The Best Poems of Tomas Tranströmer*, translated by Robert Bly. St. Paul MN: Graywolf Press, 2001. [chapter 11]

Walls, Martin. "Snail." *Third Coast*, no. 14 (Spring 2002): 45. [chapter 11]

Walsh, Marnie. "Bessie Dreaming Bear: Rosebud, So. Dak., 1960." In *A Taste of the Knife*. Boise ID: Ahsahta Press, 1976. [chapter 9]

Wayne, Jane. "When It Lifts." *American Scholar* 72, no. 4 (2003): 112. [chapter 9]

Weeks, Edward. *This Trade of Writing*. Boston: Little, Brown & Co., 1936. [chapter 1]

Weismiller, Edward. "Sea Horse." In *Walking toward the Sun*. New Haven CT: Yale University Press, 2002. Copyright (c) 2002 by Yale University. Published by permission of Yale University Press. [chapter 5]

Willard, Nancy. "Night Light." In *Household Tales of Moon and Crater*, copyright (c) 1980 by Nancy Willard, reprinted by permission of Harcourt, Inc. [chapter 12]